# A NEW OWNER'S
## GUIDE TO
# PEKINGESE

JG-157

**Overleaf:** Pekingese adult and puppies.

**Opposite page:** Dragonhai Crystabelle, owned by Nancy C. Ross

**The Publisher wishes to acknowledge the following owners of the dogs in this book:** Edie and Cliff Jones, Rose A. Marchetti, Celia Ooi, Prairie Breeze Pekingese, Nancy C. Ross, Nancy H. Shapland, Anne E. Snelling, and Tan Yin Ying.

**Photographers:** Ashbey Photography, Isabelle Francais, Edie and Cliff Jones, Rose A. Marchetti, Celia Ooi, Robert Pearcy, Pets By Paulette, Prairie Breeze Pekingese, Nancy C. Ross, Robert Smith, Vince Serbin, and Tan Yin Ying.

The author acknowledges the contribution of Judy Iby to the following chapters: Health Care, Sport of Purebred Dogs, Identification and Finding the Lost Dog, Traveling with Your Dog, and Behavior and Canine Communication.

The portrayal of canine pet products in this book is for general instructive value only; the appearance of such products does not necessarily constitute an endorsement by the authors, the publisher, or the owners of the dogs portrayed in this book.

## © T.F.H. Publications, Inc.

Distributed in the UNITED STATES to the Pet Trade by T.F.H. Publications, Inc., One T.F.H. Plaza, Neptune City, NJ 07753; on the Internet at www.tfh.com; in CANADA Rolf C. Hagen Inc., 3225 Sartelon St. Laurent-Montreal Quebec H4R 1E8; Pet Trade by H & L Pet Supplies Inc., 27 Kingston Crescent, Kitchener, Ontario N2B 2T6; in ENGLAND by T.F.H. Publications, PO Box 74, Havant PO9 5TT; in AUSTRALIA AND THE SOUTH PACIFIC by T.F.H. (Australia), Pty. Ltd., Box 149, Brookvale 2100 N.S.W., Australia; in NEW ZEALAND by Brooklands Aquarium Ltd. 5 McGiven Drive, New Plymouth, RD1 New Zealand; in SOUTH AFRICA, Rolf C. Hagen S.A. (PTY.) LTD. P.O. Box 201199, Durban North 4016, South Africa; in Japan by T.F.H. Publications, Japan—Jiro Tsuda, 10-12-3 Ohjidai, Sakura, Chiba 285, Japan. Published by T.F.H. Publications, Inc.

MANUFACTURED IN THE
UNITED STATES OF AMERICA
BY T.F.H. PUBLICATIONS, INC.

# A NEW OWNER'S
## GUIDE TO
# PEKINGESE

## DeAnn and Larry Ulmer

# Contents

6 · History and Origin of the Pekingese
The Pekingese in Legend • The Franco-British Invasion • The Pekingese in America

12 · Characteristics of the Pekingese
Think Carefully About Dog Ownership • The Case for Purebred Dogs • Life with a Pekingese • Male or Female? • The Pekingese Personality

**Choose a puppy that is alert and active, with bright eyes and a shining coat.**

24 · Standard for the Pekingese
Revised Standard for the Pekingese

30 · Selecting the Right Pekingese for You
Where to Buy Your Pekingese • Recognizing a Healthy Puppy • Selecting a Puppy • Selecting a Show-Prospect Puppy • Puppy or Adult? • Identification Papers Diet Sheet • Health Guarantee • Temperament and Socialization • The Adolescent Pekingese

**The Pekingese has a regal and majestic bearing.**

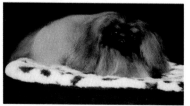

50 · Caring for Your Pekingese
Feeding and Nutrition • Special Needs of the Pekingese • Common Sense

60 · Grooming Your Pekingese
Regular Coat Care • Bathing

70 · Housebreaking and Training Your Pekingese
Housebreaking • Basic Training • Versatility

88 · Sport of Purebred Dogs
Puppy Kindergarten • Conformation • Canine Good Citizen • Obedience • Agility • Performance Tests • General Information

**This lovely pair of Pekingese pose for posterity.**

136 · Identification and Finding the Lost Dog
Finding The Lost Dog

140 · Behavior and Canine Communication
Canine Behavior • Socializing and Training • Understanding the Dog's Language • Body Language • Fear • Aggression • Problems

106 · Health Care
The First Checkup • The Physical Examination • Immunizations • Annual Visits • Intestinal Parasites • Other Internal Parasites External Parasites • To Breed or Not to Breed • Medical Problems

124 · Dental Care for Your Dog's Life

128 · Traveling with Your Dog
Trips • Air Travel • Boarding Kennels

**This little Peke puppy looks ready for a little mischief!**

159 · Suggested Reading

160 · Index

**The Pekingese's loving and happy disposition makes him the ideal family pet.**

# HISTORY and Origin of the Pekingese

Mankind's love of dogs extends back into the earliest mists of time when wolf and human met and took the first steps on a mutual journey toward civilization and companionship. That *Canis Lupus,* the wolf, traveled alongside man on this path is an historical fact. Moreover, it is man himself who can be credited for the wolf's journey from creature of the forest to *Canis familiaris,* the domesticated dog.

Companion and purely ornamental Toy breeds are known to have existed even before dynastic times in Egypt. Pictures of very small, lightly colored dogs with silken coats appear on urns and vases excavated from the ruins of ancient Greece. These dogs are thought to be descendants of a northern, more wolf-like dog that developed as early as Neolithic times and resembled today's spitz-type breeds.

Extensive research has been done by canine historians Richard and Alice Fiennes into the development of the individual canine breeds, the results of which can be found in their excellent book, *The Natural History of Dogs.* They are convinced that the small, companion-type dogs of Egypt also existed throughout the Roman Empire and accompanied the caravans and trading ships to Tibet.

The Tibetans at that time enjoyed trade with China, and there is no doubt that the little dogs that had made their way from Egypt

*The diminutive Pekingese has an illustrious history, dating back to the days of the ancient Chinese dynasties.*

*Although it may seem unlikely when looking at the little Pekingese, the domesticated dogs of today all share the wolf as their common ancestor.*

to Rome and on to Tibet also had influence in the development of China's *ha pa* dogs. The term *ha pa*, translated to "under the table dogs," has particular significance in that it relates to dogs that were small enough to fit under the tables used in China, that at the time were only about eight inches high. It is highly likely that these *ha pa* dogs made their way back along the caravan routes to Tibet and influenced dogs there as well.

## The Pekingese in Legend

An ancient Chinese legend makes the origin of the Pekingese a romantic tale indeed. It is said that many centuries ago, a lion met and fell in love with a marmoset. Due to the lion's large size, the two were obviously incompatible. In order to have his beloved, the lion sacrificed his size, but not his courage or great heart. The loving pair was thus able to form an alliance, and from the two came the offspring that were the first Pekingese. To this day, the Peke retains his diminutive stature and lion-sized courage.

Although it is unlikely that this beautiful tale is based in reality, it is the Chinese love of beauty and perfection to which the Pekingese owes his development. The opulence of the Chinese courts made way for time and resources to be directed toward development and appreciation of all things beautiful. No study of Chinese art could help but lead the student to realize that the exotic little dogs developed there can be compared to the exquisite detail found in silk painting, embroidery, and porcelain art. There are few, if any, other breeds that can match the level of development achieved by the Pekingese, or maintain it over such a long period of time.

The arts, of which the little lion dogs were a part, were entrusted to the eunuchs and women of the palace courts. They competed to outdo each other in order to gain the special favor of the emperors. Moreover, it is believed that the various exotic colors of the Pekingese breed were developed as a result of this competition.

*The Pekingese dog existed for over 2,000 years in China before being introduced to Europe in the late 19th century.*

In the time of the Ming dynasty, the dogs, along with other art treasures, were housed in the royal Summer Palace that was situated a short distance from the Forbidden City of Peking. The Ming Dynasty had achieved such an absolute level of rule that there was no act, regardless of how unfair, treacherous, or cruel, that could be questioned.

The famous Dowager Empress Tzu Hsi was a great champion of the Pekingese breed, but her despotic rule was no exception to her predecessors. There was no doubt of her cruelty or the high level of hatred she bore for the West. Her love of the breed and her cruelty toward others can be seen in the sanctions and terrible punishments she inflicted upon those who attempted to remove a Pekingese from the royal palace. Stoning to death, or "death by a thousand slices," were fates thieves were sure to incur.

*Their nickname, the little lion dog, stems from the myth of the Pekingese's origins.*

### THE FRANCO-BRITISH INVASION

The trade restrictions imposed by the Empress on the rest of the world were intolerable. Nor did she spare any effort in inspiring the entire Chinese population's hatred of the Europeans. She made it very clear that she would do all in her power to drive the "foreign devils" out of the country.

Her hatred led to the first China War of 1860 which, to her dismay, led to the eventual downfall of the dynasty. France and Britain invaded China and eventually reached the Imperial City of Peking itself.

During the invasion and looting of the Summer Palace, three officers of the British troops, Lord John Hay, Lieutenant Dunne, and Sir George Fitzroy, came upon five of the treasured "little lion dogs" and returned to England with the exotic dogs. After 2,000 years of breeding in China, the Pekingese made his entrance into Western civilization. The five dogs are the direct ancestors of many Pekingese in England today.

Two of the dogs were given to the Dutchess of Richmond and Gordon. Lord Hay had two others; a dog named Schlorff, who lived to be 18 years old, and a female, Hytien, whom he gave to his sister. The fifth dog of the quintet, a parti-color female named Looty, was given to Queen Victoria by Lieutenant Dunne.

The breed's distinctive appearance, and the fact that the Queen had developed such a fondness for her Looty, inspired interest in the diminutive Orientals. Interest grew rapidly.

Increased demand created a need for importing the dogs directly from China. The changing political climate there allowed the dogs to be given as gifts to the honored few in Great Britain. If one judges by the rapid increase of numbers in the West, many imports arrived that were never recorded and of which nothing is known.

*The Pekingese made his first appearance in the United States in the early 20th century.*

By the first decade of the present century, England had replaced China as the home of the Pekingese. The Pekingese Club was formed in 1902, and by 1919, it had become the number-one registered dog by The Kennel Club in England.

*The Pekingese is a wonderful dog that inspires lifelong devotion in those who own him.*

## THE PEKINGESE IN AMERICA

The first classes for the "Pekingese Spaniel," as he was called then, were offered by the Toy Spaniel Club in 1906. T'ang of Downshire was selected as Best of Breed at that show, and the dog went on to become the first champion of record registered by the American Kennel Club. Chaou Ching-Ur, a female that had been bred by Tzu Hsi, the Dowager Empress herself, followed him to the title.

In 1909, the Pekingese Club of America was formed, and the organization held its own first specialty show in 1911 with 95 dogs entered. The event was held at the Plaza Hotel in New York, and there is little doubt that the considerable coverage the glittering event gained from eastern newspapers was due to the interest the breed had achieved among society notables. The list of exhibitors and spectators could well have been a page torn from the social register. The Pekingese's permanent position on the American dog scene was well established.

American interest in the Pekingese has remained constant and grown slowly and steadily over the past century. Fortunately for the breed, Pekes never became a fad, and thus avoided the pitfalls so many overly popular breeds have had to endure.

In 1997, there were approximately 13,000 Pekingese registered with the American Kennel Club. That number placed the breed in 27th position among the 145 breeds recognized by the AKC. .

# CHARACTERISTICS of the Pekingese

## THINK CAREFULLY ABOUT DOG OWNERSHIP

**B**efore anyone tries to decide whether the Pekingese is the correct breed for him or her, a larger, more important question must be asked. That question is, "Should I own a dog at all?" Dog ownership is a serious and time-consuming responsibility that should not be entered into lightly. Failure to understand this can make what should be a rewarding relationship instead one of sheer drudgery, particularly in the case of a coated breed. It is also one of the primary reasons why thousands upon thousands of unwanted dogs end up in humane societies and animal shelters throughout America each year.

If the prospective dog owner lives alone and conditions are conducive to dog ownership, all he or she needs to do is be sure that there is a strong desire to make the

*A Pekingese dog may be irresistible, but be certain to educate yourself about the responsibilities of owning a dog before you bring one home.*

*The Pekingese has a number of unique qualities that make him a versatile and amiable breed.*

necessary commitment dog ownership entails. In the case of family households, the situation is a much more complicated one. It is vital that the person who will actually be responsible for the dog's care really wants a dog.

In many households, mothers are most often given the additional responsibility of caring for the family pets. Children are away at school all day. Father is at work. Often it is the mother, even the working mother, who is saddled with the additional chores of housebreaking, feeding, and trips to the veterinary hospital with what was supposed to be a family project.

Most children love puppies and dogs and will promise anything to get one. However, childhood enthusiasm can wane very quickly and it will be up to the adults in the family to ensure the dog receives proper care. It is important that children are taught responsibility but to expect a living, breathing, and needy animal to teach a child this lesson is incredibly indifferent to the needs of the animal.

There are also many households from which the entire family is gone from early morning until late in the day. The question that must be asked then is: Who will provide food for the dog and access to the out-of-doors if the dog is expected not to relieve himself in the house? This is something that can probably be worked out with an adult dog of most any breed, but it is totally unfair for anyone to expect a young puppy to be left alone the entire day.

Should an individual or family find that they are capable of providing the proper home for a dog or young puppy, suitability of breed must also be considered. Here it might be worthwhile to look at the difference between owning a purebred dog and one of mixed ancestry.

### THE CASE FOR PUREBRED DOGS

A mongrel can give you as much love and devotion as a purebred dog. However, the manner in which the dog does this and how his personality, energy level, and the amount of care he requires suits an individual's lifestyle are major considerations. In a purebred dog, most of these considerations are predictable to a marked degree, even if the dog is purchased as a very young puppy. A puppy of uncertain parentage will not give you this assurance.

All puppies are cute and manageable, but someone who lives in a two-room apartment will find life difficult with a dog that grows to the size of a Great Dane. Nor is the mountain climber or marathon runner going to be happy with a short-nosed breed that has difficulty catching his breath while simply walking across the street on a hot summer day.

One who expects a dog to sit quietly by their owner's side while he or she watches television or reads is not going to be particularly happy with a high-strung, off-the-wall dog whose rest requirements are only 30 seconds out of every ten hours! The outdoorsman is not going to be particularly happy with a long-coated breed that attracts every burr, leaf, and insect in all of nature.

Knowing what kind of dog best suits your lifestyle is not just a consideration. It is paramount to the foundation of your lifelong relationship with the dog. If the dog you are considering does not fit your lifestyle, the relationship simply will not last.

## LIFE WITH A PEKINGESE

All of the foregoing points apply to whether you should own a Pekingese. Further, though an adorable Pekingese puppy has a certain greeting-card appeal, he is a long-coated dog that needs a great deal of care! Daily brushing and frequent bathing is necessary. When the Pekingese is outdoors, he is no less a dog than any other. He enjoys playing in the mud, burying himself in the sandbox, or rolling in the brambles as much as a dog of any other breed would. This must be dealt with immediately.

The Pekingese is a long-coated breed that will only stay healthy and looking like a Pekingese as long as you are willing to invest the time in keeping it that way. If you do not feel you have the time to do this yourself, it will be necessary to have a professional groomer do this for

*The Pekingese's loving and happy disposition makes him a welcome addition to most families.*

you. If you appreciate the look of the breed, realize that it will take more than a little effort on your part to keep it looking that way.

If you are willing to make the necessary commitment that a Pekingese requires, let us assure you there are few breeds that are any more amiable and adaptable. While the Pekingese may well have been the pampered pet of the emperors and carried around on a royal cushion, don't misunderstand these little tykes!

*Personalities will vary among Pekingese, so be sure to choose one that will fit with your lifestyle.*

Pekes are independent creatures who definitely have their own mind! Although this can be exasperating at times, it is easily mitigated by the fact that they are one of the most intelligent, loving, and human-like canines we know. He is a breed that so endears himself to you that few people are happy without one in their home.

The Peke is playful and loves to be snuggled, but they are not obsessively dependent dogs. They can be left home alone for reasonable periods of time without becoming stressed. Most Pekingese seem to enjoy the company of other Pekes, and this is definitely one of those breeds that fall into the "two dogs are better than one" category.

*This little Pekingese lady has no doubt about her loyal ancestry!*

Pekes keep each other company, and some of our own most enjoyable hours are the ones we have spent watching our Pekes play and interact. They wrestle and chase each other about just like children.

None of this should minimize the breed's inherent stubbornness. Those of us who show our Pekes know very well what a nightmare a stubborn Peke can be. If a Peke has made up his mind that he will not walk in the show ring, you may as well accept it. This applies around the home as well. Sometimes, early training and a lot of socialization can help, but patience is vital.

Pekingese are very protective of their family and make good guard dogs in that no intruder will ever enter their domain without being noticed or having the alarm sounded. Still, the Peke is not a noisy dog. They save their bark for when it counts. Without a doubt, he is a courageous and sturdy little dog with a heart that exceeds the casing in which he is kept.

The breed is a hardy one and, if purchased from a responsible breeder, is seldom prone to chronic illnesses. The

Pekingese is of a diminutive size, but that does not mean he must be treated as if made of eggshells. For his size, the Peke has amazing energy and great strength. With proper instruction, children old enough to understand how to handle a small dog can learn to enjoy the exuberant personality of the Pekingese, and the Peke, in turn, will love the gentle child.

## MALE OR FEMALE?

While the sex of a dog in many breeds is a very important consideration, this is not particularly the case with the Pekingese. The male Pekingese makes just as loving, devoted, and trainable companion as the female. In fact, there are some who believe a male can be even more devoted to his master.

There is one important point to consider in determining your choice between male and female. While both must be trained not to relieve themselves in the home, males have a natural instinct to lift their leg and urinate to "mark" their home territory. It seems confusing to many dog owners, but a male's marking of his home turf has absolutely nothing to do with whether or not he is housebroken. The two responses come from entirely different needs and must be dealt with in that manner. Some dogs are more difficult than others are to train not to mark within the confines of the household. Males that are used for breeding are more prone to this response and even harder to break of doing so.

On the other hand, females have their semiannual heat cycles once they have reached sexual maturity. In the case of the female Pekingese, this can occur for the first time at about

*This relaxed, nonchalant little fellow may seem reserved at first, but once you win his affection, he will become very attached to his loved ones.*

nine or ten months of age. These cycles are accompanied by a vaginal discharge that creates the need to confine the female for about three weeks so that she does not soil her surroundings. It must be understood that the female has no control over this bloody discharge. It has nothing to do with training.

*This adorable Peke puppy is the perfect example of good breeding!*

While most Pekingese are not normally left outdoors by themselves for long stretches, this is one time a female should not be out by herself, even for a brief moment or two. The need for confinement and keeping a careful watch over the female in heat is especially important to protect her from some neighborhood Lothario. Especially dangerous to your female's well-being is the male that is much larger than she is. The dog may be too large to actually breed her, but he could seriously injure or even kill her in his attempts to do so.

*Whether male or female, the Pekingese will make an equally loving, devoted, and trainable companion.*

*Despite his small size, the Pekingese enjoys an occasional playful romp in the great outdoors.*

These sexually related problems can be eliminated by spaying the female and neutering the male. Unless a Pekingese has been purchased expressly for breeding or showing from a breeder capable of making this judgment, your dog should be sexually altered.

The breeding and raising of Pekingese puppies should be left in the hands of people who have the necessary experience to deal with the many difficulties involved. The Pekingese is one of the most difficult breeds from which to whelp and raise puppies. The pups are born with large heads, therefore, costly caesarean sections are performed frequently. Breeding Pekes is an expensive proposition, and at times can be very traumatic and heartbreaking. It is best left to those who have been through the ordeal many times.

Then, too, very few single dog owners have the facilities or time necessary to keep each and every puppy they breed until the correct home is found for him. This can often take many months after the puppies are born. Naturally, a responsible Pekingese owner would never allow his or her pet to roam the streets and end his life in an animal shelter. Unfortunately, being forced to place a puppy due to space constraints before you are able to thoroughly check out the prospective buyer may, in fact, create this exact situation.

Many times, parents ask to buy a female "just as a pet" but with the full intention of breeding so that their children can witness the birth process. There are countless books and videos now available that portray this wonderful event and do not add to the worldwide pet overpopulation we now face. Altering one's companion dogs not only precludes the possibility of adding to this problem, it eliminates bothersome household problems and precautions.

*Although it may take time and patience, your Pekingese is very intelligent and can be trained to do almost anything.*

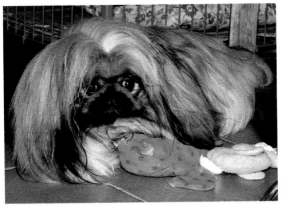

It should be understood, however, that spaying and neutering are not reversible procedures. Spayed females or neutered males are not allowed to be shown in American Kennel Club shows, nor will altered animals ever be able to be used for breeding.

### THE PEKINGESE PERSONALITY

Historically, the Pekingese has been a close companion of man. Whether the pampered treasure of the royal courts or a traveler abroad, everything the Pekingese has done has been in the company of humans. He is happiest when allowed to continue the association. It simply would not do for a Pekingese to be shut away in a kennel or run with only occasional access to your life and environment. Should this be your intent, you would be better served by another breed. The very essence of the Pekingese is in his unique personality and sensitive and loving nature, which is best developed by constant human contact.

None of this should be construed to mean that only people who are home all day to cater to every whim of their dog can be a Pekingese owner. We know many working people who are away most of the day whose Pekingese are well mannered and trustworthy when left home alone. The key here seems to be the quality rather than the quantity of time spent with their pet. Morning or evening walks, grooming sessions, game time, and simply having your Pekingese share your life when you are home is vital to the breed's personality development and attitude. A Pekingese likes to be talked to and praised. Like the old adage, "no man is an island," this applies to dogs as well, particularly so in the case of the Pekingese.

We have never seen a Pekingese even indicate he would challenge his owner on any point, regardless of how much he might object to what he is being asked

*Dedicated Pekingese breeders are careful to be true to the breed's original character and purpose.*

to do. A Peke might absolutely refuse to do something but seldom, if ever, would he turn on his owner or family. Therefore, a stern and disapproving voice is usually more than sufficient to let your Pekingese know that you do not approve of what he is doing. It is never necessary to strike a Pekingese in any circumstance. A sharp "no" is normally more than it takes to make your point.

Many Pekingese owners are inclined to think of their companions as "little people," but it must be understood that the Pekingese is first a *dog*. Dogs, like the wolves from which they descend, are pack animals and they need a "pack leader." Dogs are now totally dependent upon humans to provide that leadership. When that leadership is not provided, a dog can easily become confused and neurotic.

Setting boundaries is important to the well-being of your Pekingese and your relationship to him. The sooner your dog understands that rules must be obeyed, the easier it will be for him to become an enjoyable companion. The time you take to establish and enforce those rules will determine how quickly this will come about. As we mentioned earlier, the Pekingese is not vindictive or particularly stubborn, but he does need guidance in order to achieve his potential.

# STANDARD for the Pekingese

The Board of Directors of the American Kennel Club has approved the following revised standard for the Pekingese as submitted by the Pekingese Club of America, Inc.

## General Appearance

The Pekingese is a well-balanced, compact dog with heavy front and lighter hindquarters. It must suggest his Chinese origin in his directness, independence, individuality, and expression. His image is lionlike. It should imply courage, boldness and self-esteem rather than prettiness, daintiness or delicacy.

## Size, Substance, Proportion

*Size/Substance*—The Pekingese should be surprisingly heavy when lifted. He has a stocky, muscular body. The bone of the forequarters must be very heavy in relation to the size of the dog. All weights are correct within the limit of 14 pounds, provided that type and points are not sacrificed. *Disqualification: weight over 14 pounds. Proportion*—The length of the body, from the front of the breast bone in a straight line to the buttocks, is slightly greater than the height at the withers. Overall balance is of utmost importance.

## Head

*Skull*—The topskull is massive, broad and flat (not dome-shaped). The topskull, the high, wide cheek bones, broad lower jaw and wide chin are the structural formation of the correctly shaped face. When viewed

*Although small, the Pekingese is a well-balanced and compact dog.*

*The Pekingese has a pleasing expression—it should imply courage, boldness, and self-esteem.* frontally, the skull is wider than deep and contributes to the rectangular envelope-shaped appearance of the head. In profile, the Pekingese face must be flat. The chin, nose leather and brow all lie in one plane. In the natural position of the head, this plane appears vertical but slants very slightly backward from chin to forehead. *Nose*—It is black, broad, very short and in profile, contributes to the flat appearance of the face. Nostrils are open. The nose is positioned between the eyes so that a line drawn horizontally across the top of the nose intersects the center of the eyes. *Eyes*—They are large, very dark, round, lustrous and set wide apart. The look is bold, not bulging. The eye rims are black and the white of the eye does not show when the dog is looking straight ahead. *Wrinkle*—It effectively separates the upper and lower areas of the face. The appearance is of a hair covered fold of skin, extending from one cheek, over the bridge of the nose in a wide inverted "V", to the other cheek. It is NEVER so prominent or heavy as to crowd the facial features nor to obscure a large portion of the eyes or the nose from view. *Stop*—It is deep. The bridge of the nose is completely obscured from view by hair and/or the over-nose wrinkle. *Muzzle*—This is very short and broad with high, wide cheek bones. The color of the skin is black. Whiskers add to the Oriental expression. *Mouth*—The lower jaw is slightly undershot. The lips meet on a level plane and neither teeth nor tongue show when the mouth is closed. The lower jaw is strong, wide, firm and straight across at the chin. An excessively strong chin is as undesirable as a weak one. *Ears*—They are heart-shaped and set on the front corners of the skull extending the line of the topskull. Correctly placed ears frame the sides of the face and with their heavy feathering create an illusion of additional width of the head. *Pigment*—The skin of the nose, lips and eye rims is black on all colors.

## Neck, Body, Tail

*Neck*—It is very short, thick and set back into the shoulder. *Body*—This is pear-shaped and compact. It is heavy in front with well-sprung ribs slung between the forelegs. The broad chest, with little or no protruding breast bone, tapers to lighter loins with a distinct waist. The topline is level. *Tail*—The base is set high; the remainder is carried well over the center of the back. Long, profuse straight feathering may fall to either side.

*The Pekingese's tail should be set on high and carried erect.*

## Forequarters

They are short, thick and heavy-boned. The bones of the forelegs are slightly bowed between the pastern and elbow. Shoulders are gently laid back and fit smoothly into the body. The elbows are always close to the body. Front feet are large, flat and turned slightly out. The dog must stand well up on feet.

*The Pekingese's coat should be full-bodied, long, and coarse, with a thick, soft undercoat.*

*The Pekingese temperament is an interesting combination of dignity, self importance, confidence, and stubbornness.*

## Hindquarters

They are lighter in bone than the forequarters. There is moderate angulation and definition of stifle and hock. When viewed from behind, the rear legs are reasonably close and parallel and the feet point straight ahead.

**Soundness is essential in both forequarters and hindquarters.**

## Coat

*Body Coat*—It is full-bodied, with long, coarse textured, straight, stand-off coat and thick, softer undercoat. The coat forms a noticeable mane on the neck and shoulder area with the coat on the remainder of the body somewhat shorter in length. A long and profuse coat is desirable providing that it does not obscure the shapeliness of the body, nor sacrifice the correct coat texture. *Feathering*—Long feathering is found on the back of the thighs and forelegs, and on the ears, tail and toes. The feathering is left on the toes but should not be so long as to prevent free movement.

## Color

All coat colors and markings, including parti-colors, are allowable and of equal merit.

## Gait

The gait is unhurried and dignified, with a slight roll over the shoulders. The rolling gait is caused by the bowed front legs and heavier, wider forequarters pivoting on the tapered waist and the lighter, straight parallel hindquarters. The rolling motion is smooth and effortless and is as free as possible from bouncing, prancing or jarring.

## Temperament

A combination of regal dignity, self-importance, self-confidence, and exasperating stubbornness make for a good natured, lively, and affectionate companion to those who have earned his respect.

**The foregoing is a description of the ideal Pekingese. Any deviation should be penalized in direct proportion to the extent of that deviation.**

**FAULTS TO BE NOTED**

Dudley, Liver or Gray Nose.
Light Brown, Yellow or Blue Eyes.
Protruding Tongue or Teeth.
Overshot Upper Jaw.
Wry Mouth.
Ears Set Much Too High, Low or Far Back.
Roach or Swayback.
Straight-Boned Forelegs.

Points:

Expression` ........................................................ 5
Nose ................................................................. 5
Stop ................................................................. 5
Muzzle .............................................................. 5
Legs and Feet ..................................................... 15
Tail ................................................................. 5
Skull ............................................................... 10
Eyes ................................................................. 5
Ears ................................................................. 5
Shape of Body .................................................... 20
Coat, Feather & Condition ..................................... 10
Action. ............................................................ 10

Total ............................. 100

*The coat of the Pekingese may consist of a number of colors and markings, including parti-color.*

*Disqualification: weight over 14 pounds.*

Approved June 13, 1995
Effective July 31, 1995

# SELECTING the Right Pekingese for You

The Pekingese you buy will live with you for many years to come. It is not unusual for the well-bred Pekingese to live as long as 12, 14, or 15 years of age. Obviously, it is important that the Pekingese you select has the advantage of beginning life in a healthy environment and comes from sound, healthy stock.

The only way you can be sure of this is to go directly to a breeder who has earned a reputation over the years for consistently producing Pekingese that are mentally and physically sound. The best way a breeder can earn this reputation is by following a well-planned breeding program that has been governed by rigid selectivity. Selective breeding programs are aimed at maintaining the many fine qualities of the Pekingese and eliminating any genetic weaknesses.

This process is both time consuming and costly for a breeder, but it ensures the buyer of getting a dog that will be a joy to own. Responsible Pekingese breeders protect their investment by basing their breeding programs on the healthiest, most representative stock available, and providing each succeeding generation with the very best care and nutrition.

The governing kennel clubs of the world maintain lists of local breed clubs and breeders that can lead a prospective Pekingese buyer to responsible breeders of quality stock. If you are not sure of where to contact an established Pekingese breeder in your area, we strongly recommend contacting a kennel club or a local Pekingese club for recommendations. Check your newspapers for announcements of local dog shows and speak to the Pekingese exhibitors there. You are bound to get recommendations from them.

It is very likely that you will be able to find an established Pekingese breeder in your own area. If so, you will be able to visit the breeder, inspect the premises and, in most cases, see a puppy's parents and other relatives. Certainly, the mother of the puppies should be on the premises.

Seeing first hand the environment in which your puppy was born and raised will tell you a great deal about what you can expect your puppy's constitution to be like as he matures.

If there are no breeders in your immediate area, you can arrange to have a puppy shipped to you. There are breeders throughout the country that have shipped puppies to satisfied owners out of state and even to other countries. However, it is extremely important that you ask questions and check the references of any kennel you cannot visit personally.

*These tiny Pekingese are only hours old. Healthy puppies are plump and content right from birth.*

Never hesitate to ask the breeder you visit or deal with any questions or concerns you might have relative to owning a Pekingese. You should expect the breeder to ask you a good number of questions as well. Good breeders are just as interested in placing their puppies in a loving and safe environment as you are in obtaining a happy, healthy puppy.

A good Pekingese breeder will want to know if there are young children in the family and what their ages are. They will also want to know if you or your children have ever owned a dog before. The breeder will want to know if you live in an apartment or in a home. If in a home, they will want to know if you have a fenced yard and if there will be someone home during the day to attend to a young puppy's needs.

Not all good breeders maintain large kennels. In fact, you are more apt to find that Pekingese come from the homes of small hobby breeders who only keep a few dogs and have litters occasionally. The names of these people are just as likely to appear on the recommended lists from kennel clubs as from the larger kennels that maintain many dogs. Hobby breeders are equally dedicated to breeding quality Pekingese, and have the distinct advantage of being able to raise their puppies in the home environment, with all the accompanying personal attention and socialization.

Again, it is important that both the buyer and the seller ask questions. We would be highly suspect of a person who is willing to sell you a Pekingese puppy with no questions asked.

### RECOGNIZING A HEALTHY PUPPY

Most Pekingese breeders are apt to keep their puppies until they are 12 to 14 weeks of age and have been given all of their puppy inoculations. By the time the litter is eight weeks of age, it is entirely weaned and no longer nursing on its mother. While the puppies were nursing, they had complete immunity from diseases from their mother. Once they stop nursing, however, they become highly susceptible to many infectious diseases. A number of these diseases can

*Be sure to do your homework and learn all you can about the breed before making the decision to bring a Pekingese into your home.*

*Like mother, like daughter! Often the temperament of a puppy will be much like her parents.*

be transmitted from the hands and clothing of humans. Therefore, it is extremely important that your puppy is current on all the shots he must have for his age.

## SELECTING A PUPPY

A healthy Pekingese puppy is a bouncy, playful extrovert. Never select a puppy that appears shy or listless because you feel sorry for it. Doing so will undoubtedly lead to heartache and expensive veterinary costs. Do not attempt to make up for what the breeder did not do in providing the proper care and nutrition. It seldom works.

If possible, take the Pekingese puppy you are attracted to into a different room of the kennel or house. The smells will remain the same for the puppy, so he should still feel secure. This will give you an opportunity to see how the puppy acts away from his littermates, and it will also give you time to inspect the puppy more closely. Sit on the floor so that you are at the puppy's level, have treats, and make friends.

Although Pekingese puppies are very small, they should feel sturdy to the touch. They should not feel bony, nor should their abdomens be bloated and extended. A puppy that has just eaten may have a full belly, but he should never appear obese.

A healthy puppy's ears will be pink and clean. Dark discharge or a bad odor could be an indication of ear mites, a sure sign of lack of cleanliness and poor maintenance. A Pekingese puppy's breath should always smell sweet. His teeth must be clean and bright, and there should never be any malformation of the jaw, lips, or nostrils.

Pekingese eyes should be dark and clear, and although they are large, they should never appear bulging or unattractive. Runny eyes, or eyes that appear red and irritated, could be caused by a myriad of problems, none of which indicate a healthy puppy.

Coughing or diarrhea are danger signals, as are any discharge from the nose or eruptions on the skin. The skin should be clean, and the coat soft, clean, and lustrous.

The puppy's attitude tells you a great deal about his state of health. Puppies that are feeling "out of sorts" react very quickly and will usually find a warm littermate to snuggle with, and will prefer to stay that way even when the rest of the gang wants to play or go exploring. The Pekingese is an extrovert. Do not settle for anything less in selecting your puppy.

## SELECTING A SHOW-PROSPECT PUPPY

If you or your family are considering a show career for your puppy, we strongly advise putting yourself in the hands of an

*Choosing a male or female puppy is a matter of preference, either sex will make a wonderful companion.*

established breeder who has earned a reputation for breeding winning show dogs. They alone are most capable of anticipating what one might expect a young puppy of their line to develop into when he reaches maturity.

Although the potential buyer should read the American Kennel Club standard of perfection for the Pekingese, it is hard for the novice to really understand the nuances of what is being asked for. The experienced breeder is best equipped to do so and will be happy to assist you in your quest. Even at that, no one can make accurate predictions or guarantees on a very young puppy.

*He may be tiny now, but this little Pekingese will attain most of his adult size by six months of age.*

*Puppyhood is the easiest age to socialize and train your Pekingese.*

Any predictions a breeder is apt to make are based upon the breeder's experience with past litters that produced winning show dogs. It should be obvious

that the more successful a breeder has been in producing winning Pekingese through the years, the more broad his or her basis of comparison will be.

The most any responsible breeder will say about a 12-week-old puppy is that he has "show potential." If you are serious about showing your Pekingese we, like most other breeders, strongly suggest waiting until a puppy is from 6 to 12 months old before making any decisions. It only makes sense to assume that the older the puppy, the easier it will be to determine how he will turn out.

*There is no telling what life has in store for the Pekingese you choose— he may be a champion or companion—but he'll definitely be your best friend!*

There are many other "beauty point" shortcomings a Pekingese puppy might have that would in no way interfere with him being a wonderful companion, but these faults would be serious drawbacks in the show ring. Many of these flaws are such that a beginner in the breed would hardly notice. Things such as one or no testicles for a male, an incorrect topline, or very low tail set would not keep your Pekingese from being a happy, healthy, and loving companion but would keep him from being a winner. This is why employing the assistance of a good breeder is so important. Still, the prospective buyer needs to be at least generally aware of what the Pekingese show puppy should look like.

All of the above points regarding soundness and health of the pet puppy apply to the show puppy as well. The show prospect must not only be sound and healthy, he must adhere

*Your Pekingese will look to you, his owner, to provide for all his needs.*

to the standard of the breed very closely.

The complete standard of the breed appears in another section of this book, and there are a number of other books that can assist the newcomer in learning more about the Pekingese. The more you know about the history and origin of the breed, the better equipped you will be to see the differences that distinguish the show dog from the pet.

The head of the Pekingese constitutes a good 40 percent of the breed standard, therefore it is something that must be looked at very closely. Large, dark eyes are very important. Look for a nose that has open nostrils and is placed between the eyes. Look for dark pigment. Ears are set to the sides of the flat-top skull—not too high or too far back, but framing the face. There is a wide, undershot jaw. An unbroken wrinkle extends up above the nose.

The neck should be short and thick. The ribs should be well sprung, with a broad chest. The body is constructed lion-like, heavier in front and lighter in the rear. The back should be level and the body should not be long. A high tail set is very important to the overall look of a Pekingese.

Legs are short, with the bones of the forearm bowed but

firmly attached at the shoulder. The hind legs are lighter, but firm and well shaped, and they are moderately angulated. The front feet should turn slightly outward.

The coat is like frosting on the cake. It is not necessary to have a huge coat in order to have a good dog, but a well-coated dog is a plus in the show ring.

Pekes come in many colors and all are allowed in the ring. A white, black, or parti-color Peke may not be the best choice for the beginner because it does appear to be harder to win with those colors. However, the color would make no difference to breeder judges on an otherwise good dog. A good Peke cannot be a bad color!

*There is nothing quite as endearing as a Pekingese puppy. However, keep in mind that taking care of a little one means a lot of time and work.*

The show puppy will move around with ease and an "I love the world" attitude. Temperament of this kind is a hallmark of the breed.

## Puppy or Adult?

For the person anticipating a show career for their Pekingese or for someone hoping to become a breeder, the purchase of a young adult provides greater certainty with respect to quality. Even those who simply want a companion could consider the adult dog.

From a breeder's point of view, Pekingese act like puppies their entire lives and readily adapt to new places and people quite easily. In some instances, breeders will have males or females they no longer wish to use for breeding, and, after the dogs have been altered, would prefer to have them live out their lives in a private home with all its attendant care and attention.

*Your Pekingese's pedigree will offer you important information about his ancestry.*

In the private home environment, the dog will become the "one and only" instead of one of many.

Acquiring an adult dog eliminates the many problems that raising a puppy involves, and Pekingese, unlike some other breeds, do transfer into a new home well. They love to be with humans, and though many of us hate to admit it, most Pekingese are just as content living with one person as they are with another, just so long as they are loved and well cared for.

Elderly people often prefer the adult dog, particularly one that is housebroken in that they are easier to manage and require less supervision or damage control. Adult Pekingese are seldom chewers, and are usually more than ready to adapt to household rules.

There are things to consider though. Adult dogs have developed behaviors that may or may not fit into your routine. If a Pekingese has never been exposed to small children, he may be totally perplexed, often frightened, by this new experience. Children are also inclined to be more active and vocal than the average adult, and this could intimidate the dog as well.

*A healthy Pekingese puppy should have bright eyes and a shiny coat.*

We strongly advise taking an adult dog on a

trial basis to see if he will adapt to the new owner's lifestyle and environment. Most often it works, but on rare occasions, a prospective owner decides that training his or her dog from puppyhood is worth the time and effort it requires.

## IDENTIFICATION PAPERS

The purchase of any purebred dog entitles you to three very important documents: a health record, which includes an inoculation or "shot" record, a copy of the dog's pedigree, and the registration certificate.

### Inoculations

You will find that most Pekingese breeders have initiated the necessary inoculation series for their puppies by the time they are 12 weeks of age. These inoculations temporarily protect the puppies against hepatitis, leptospirosis, distemper, and canine parvovirus. Permanent inoculations will follow at a prescribed time. Since different

*A pedigree will prove that the parents of your puppy are purebred Pekingese.*

breeders and veterinarians follow different approaches to inoculations, it is extremely important that the health record you obtain for your puppy accurately lists what shots have been given and when. In this way, the veterinarian you choose will be able to continue with the appropriate inoculation series as needed. In most cases, rabies inoculations are not given until a puppy is six months of age or older.

### Pedigree

The pedigree is your dog's "family tree." The breeder must supply you with a copy of this document authenticating your puppy's ancestry back to at least the third generation. All purebred dogs have pedigrees. The pedigree in itself does not mean that your puppy is of show quality. It simply means that all of his ancestors were in fact registered Pekingese. They may all have been of pet quality. Unscrupulous puppy dealers often try to imply that a pedigree indicates that all dogs having one are of championship caliber. This is not true. Again, it simply tells you that all of the dog's ancestor's are purebred.

### Registration Certificate

The registration certificate is the canine world's "birth certificate." A country's governing kennel club issues this certificate. When you transfer the ownership of your Pekingese from the breeder's name to your own, the transaction is entered on this certificate and, once mailed to the appropriate kennel club, is permanently recorded in their computerized files.

Keep all of your dog's documents in a safe place, as you will need them when you visit your veterinarian, or should you ever wish to breed or show your Pekingese. Keep the name, address, and phone number of the breeder from whom you purchased your Pekingese in a separate place as well. Should you ever lose any of these important documents, you will then

*Your Peke will soon grow into an adult diet, but during his first few weeks at your home, stick to your breeder's recommendation.*

*Your Pekingese will have a good start in life if his parents are well-adjusted. If possible, try to see the dam and sire of the puppy you are considering.*

be able to contact the breeder regarding the acquisition of duplicates.

## DIET SHEET

Your Pekingese is the happy, healthy puppy he is because the breeder has carefully fed and cared for him. Every breeder we know has his or her own particular way of doing this. Most breeders give the new owner a written record that details the amount and kind of food a puppy has been receiving. Do follow these recommendations to the letter at least for the first month or two after the puppy comes to live with you.

The diet sheet should indicate the number of times a day your Pekingese has been accustomed to being fed and the kind of vitamin supplementation, if any, he has been receiving. Following the prescribed procedure will reduce the chance of upset stomach and loose stools.

Usually a breeder's diet sheet projects the increases and changes in food that will be necessary as your puppy grows

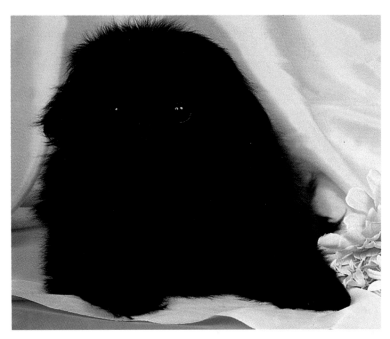

*Upon selection of your Pekingese puppy, the breeder should offer a guarantee against inherited disorders.*

from week to week. If the sheet does not include this information, ask the breeder for suggestions regarding increases and the eventual changeover to adult food.

In the unlikely event that you are not supplied with a diet sheet by the breeder and are unable to get one, your veterinarian will be able to advise you in this respect. There are countless foods now being manufactured expressly to meet the nutritional needs of puppies and growing dogs. A trip down the pet aisle at your supermarket will prove just how many choices you have. Two important tips to remember: read labels carefully for content, and when dealing with established, reliable manufacturers, you are more likely to get what you pay for. Feeding and nutrition are dealt with in detail in the chapter regarding the care of your Pekingese.

## HEALTH GUARANTEE

Any reputable breeder will be more than willing to supply a written agreement that the purchase of your Pekingese is contingent upon his passing a veterinarian's examination. Ideally, you will be able to arrange an appointment with your chosen veterinarian right after you have picked up your puppy from the breeder and before you take him home. If this is not possible, you should not delay the procedure any longer than 24 hours from the time you take your puppy home.

### TEMPERAMENT AND SOCIALIZATION

Temperament is both hereditary and environmental. Poor treatment and lack of proper socialization can ruin inherited good temperament. A Pekingese puppy that comes from shy, nervous, or aggressive stock, or one that exhibits those characteristics will make a poor companion or show dog and should certainly never be bred. Therefore, it is critical that you obtain a happy puppy from a breeder who is determined to produce good temperaments and has taken all the necessary steps to provide the early socialization necessary.

*This Pekingese obviously gets along well with other animals—even if they are only stuffed!*

Temperaments in the same litter can range from confident and outgoing on the high end of the scale to shy and fearful at the low end, but Pekingese temperament is and should be delightful. As we stated previously, this temperament is a hallmark of the breed.

Through no fault of their own, human toddlers are usually unable to understand that something as small as a Pekingese must be handled carefully. Care must always be taken that a puppy is not dropped or squeezed hard, and that he is not left to run around where he can jump from high places or a door might close on him.

If you are fortunate enough to have children in the household who are of an age capable of understanding a Pekingese puppy's needs, your socialization task will be assisted considerably. Pekingese raised with responsible children are the best. The two seem to understand each other and, in some way known only to the puppies and children themselves, they give each other the confidence to face the trying ordeal of growing up.

Every visitor that enters your household should be introduced to your Pekingese. Usually, this is completely unnecessary, as your puppy will take care of all those formalities on his own.

Your puppy should go everywhere with you—the post office, the market, the shopping mall—wherever. Be prepared to create a stir wherever you go, because the very reason that you were attracted to the first Pekingese you met applies to other people as well. Everyone will want to pet your little companion, and there is nothing in the world better for him.

Should your puppy back off from a stranger, pick him up and hand him to the person. The young Pekingese will quickly learn that all humans—young and old, short and tall, and of all races—are friends. You are in charge. You must call the shots.

If your Pekingese has a show career in his future, other things, in addition to just being handled, will have to be taught. All show dogs must learn to have their mouths inspected by the judge. The judge must also be able to check the teeth. Males must be accustomed to having their testicles touched. The dog show judge must determine that all male dogs are "complete," which means that there are two normal-sized

*The more time your dog spends with other animals, the better socialized he will become.*

46

testicles in the scrotum. These inspections must begin in puppyhood and be done on a regular and continuing basis.

Pekingese seem to be entirely compatible with other dogs as well as with humans. Their interaction with other, larger dogs must be carefully supervised, however. Other dogs are not aware of their own strength and can get entirely carried away in their enthusiasm to play. A Pekingese can incite his larger canine friend into romping and playing in a manner that might well result in an unintentional accident.

*Playfulness and activity are often signs of a healthy and well-adjusted puppy.*

*A well-socialized Pekingese will be a lifelong, loyal companion. These two young ladies pose prettily.*

## THE ADOLESCENT PEKINGESE

At any time from about six to nine months of age, the Pekingese coat begins to change. The puppy fluff will begin to be replaced by adult hair. When this happens, mats may occur where new hair growth meets already existing hair. Thorough brushing is extremely important, so it should be done every day or so to check on the coat's condition and keep it mat free.

It is important that you attend to these grooming sessions regularly during the early months of your puppy's growth. If your Pekingese has been groomed regularly as a puppy, you will find your task is much easier when you are working with the adult coat. Detailed grooming instructions are given in another section of this book.

Other physical changes will occur during this time as well. Ears on your puppy may look high, or "fly," as breeders refer to this condition. Tails can do odd things, and the well-placed and carried tail may suddenly be carried higher while the puppy is teething.

*Although the Pekingese is a relatively small dog, during adolescence he will grow in leaps and bounds!*

The adolescent Pekingese seems to grow in spurts. What once looked like a nice, compact puppy may appear short-legged and longer-bodied at six to nine months. Usually at maturity, they will regain their balanced proportions.

Food needs change during this growth period. Some Pekingese seem as if they can never get enough to eat, while others eat just enough to avoid starving. Think of Pekingese puppies as individualistic as children and act accordingly.

The amount of food you give your Pekingese should be adjusted to how much he will readily consume at each meal. If the entire meal is eaten quickly, add a small amount to the next feeding and continue to do so as the need increases. This method will ensure you of giving your puppy enough food, but you must also pay close attention to the dog's appearance and condition, as you do not want a puppy to become overweight or obese.

*When choosing your Pekingese puppy, observe him carefully. The way he behaves will tell you a lot about his temperament.*

At eight weeks of age, a Pekingese puppy is eating four meals a day. By the time he is six months old, the puppy can do well on two meals a day, with perhaps a midday snack. If your puppy does not eat the food offered, he is either not hungry or not well. Your dog will eat when he is hungry. If you suspect the dog is not well, a trip to the veterinarian is immediately in order.

This adolescent period is a particularly important one as it is the time your Pekingese must learn all the household and social rules by which he will live for the rest of his life. Your patience and commitment during this time will not only produce a respected canine good citizen, but will forge a bond between the two of you that will grow and ripen into a wonderful relationship.

# CARING for Your Pekingese

## FEEDING AND NUTRITION

The best way to make sure your Pekingese puppy is obtaining the right amount and the correct type of food for his age is to follow the diet sheet provided by the breeder from whom you obtained your puppy. Do your best not to change the puppy's diet and you will be less apt to run into digestive problems and diarrhea. Diarrhea is very serious in young puppies. Puppies with diarrhea can dehydrate very rapidly, causing severe problems and even death.

If it is necessary to change your Pekingese puppy's diet for any reason, it should be done gradually, over a period of several meals and a few days. Begin by adding a tablespoon or two of the new food, gradually increasing the amount until the meal consists entirely of the new product.

By the time your Pekingese is 10 to 12 months old, you can reduce feedings to one, or at the most two, a day. The main meal can be given either in the morning or evening. It is really a matter of choice on your part. There are two important things to remember: Feed the main meal at the same time every day, and make sure what you feed is nutritionally complete.

*A healthy Pekingese will look forward to mealtime. It seems like this little guy can't wait!*

The single meal can be supplemented by a morning or nighttime snack of hard dog biscuits made especially for small dogs. These biscuits not only become highly anticipated treats by your Pekingese, but also are genuinely helpful in maintaining healthy gums and teeth.

*Although this fuzzy bundle isn't even as large as his stuffed friends yet, puppies grow very quickly and require especially nutritious meals to grow into healthy adults.*

## Balanced Diets

In order for a canine diet to qualify as "complete and balanced" in the United States, it must meet standards set by the Subcommittee on Canine Nutrition of the National Research Council of the National Academy of Sciences. Most commercial foods manufactured for dogs meet these standards, and prove this by listing the ingredients contained in the food on every package or can. The ingredients are listed in descending order, with the main ingredient listed first.

Fed with any regularity at all, refined sugars can cause your Pekingese to become obese and will definitely create tooth decay. Candy stores do not exist in nature, and canine teeth are not genetically disposed to handling sugars. Do not feed your Pekingese candy or sweets, and avoid products that contain sugar to any high degree.

Fresh water and a properly prepared, balanced diet containing the essential nutrients, in correct proportions, are all a healthy Pekingese needs to be offered. Dog food comes canned, dry, semi-moist, "scientifically fortified," and "all-natural." A visit to your local supermarket or pet store will reveal how vast an array from which you will be able to select.

It is important to remember that all dogs, whether toy or giant, are carnivorous (meat-eating) animals. While the vegetable content of the Pekingese diet should not be overlooked, a dog's physiology and anatomy are based upon carnivorous food acquisition. Protein and fat are essential to the well-being of your Pekingese. In fact, it is wise to add a few drops of vegetable oil or bacon drippings to your dog's diet, particularly during the winter months in colder climates.

Read the list of ingredients on the package of dog food you buy. Animal protein should appear first on the label's list of ingredients. A base of quality kibble to which meat and even table scraps has been added can provide a nutritious meal for your Pekingese.

This having been said, it should be realized that in the wild, carnivores eat the entire beast they capture and kill. The carnivore's kills consist almost entirely of herbivorous (plant-eating) animals and invariably, the carnivore begins its meal with the contents of the herbivore's stomach. This provides the carbohydrates, minerals, and nutrients present in vegetables.

Through centuries of domestication, we have made our dogs entirely dependent upon us for their well-being. Therefore, we are entirely responsible for duplicating the food balance that the wild dog finds in nature. The domesticated dog's diet must include protein, carbohydrates, fats, roughage, and small amounts of essential minerals and vitamins.

Finding commercially prepared diets that contain all the necessary nutrients will not present a problem. It is important to understand, though, that these commercially prepared foods do contain most of the nutrients your Pekingese requires. Most Pekingese breeders recommend vitamin supplementation for healthy coat and increased stamina, especially for show dogs, pregnant bitches, or very young puppies.

## Oversupplementation

A great deal of controversy exists today regarding the orthopedic problems that afflict many breeds. Some claim that these problems are entirely hereditary conditions, while many others feel they can be exacerbated by overuse of mineral and vitamin supplements for puppies. Oversupplementation is now looked upon by some breeders as a major contributor to many skeletal abnormalities found in the purebred dogs of the day. In giving vitamin supplementation, one should *never* exceed the prescribed amount. No vitamin, however, is a substitute for a nutritious balanced diet.

Pregnant and lactating bitches do require supplementation of some kind, but here again, it is not a case of "if a little is good, a lot would be a great deal better." Extreme caution is advised in this case and best discussed with your veterinarian.

If the owner of a Pekingese normally eats healthy, nutritious food, there is no reason why their dog cannot be given some table scraps. What could possibly be harmful in good nutritious food?

Table scraps should be given only as part of the dog's meal and never from the table. A Pekingese that becomes accustomed to being hand fed from the table can quickly become a real pest at mealtime. Also, dinner guests may find that the pleading stare of your little Pekingese is less than appealing when dinner is being served.

Dogs do not care if food looks like a hot dog or a piece of cheese. Truly nutritious dog foods are seldom manufactured to look like food that appeals to humans. Dogs only care about how food smells and tastes. It is highly doubtful you will be eating your dog's food, so do not waste your money on these "looks just like" products.

*It seems like this little guy must be really thirsty! It is important to provide your Pekingese with cool, clean water at all times.*

Along these lines, most of the moist or canned foods that have the look of "delicious red beef" look that way because they contain great amounts of red dyes. They should not be fed to a Pekingese! The same coloring that makes these products red will stain and discolor the Pekingese facial hair. Some breeders claim these products can also cause tearing, which could stain the entire face of your Pekingese.

To test the dye content of either canned or dry foods, place a small amount of the moistened food after it has been prepared for your dog on an absorbent towel and allow it to remain there for several hours. If the paper is stained, you can rest assured your dog's hair will be stained as well. Further, preservatives and dyes are no better for your dog than they are for you.

## Special Diets

There are many commercially prepared diets for dogs with special dietary needs. The overweight, underweight, or geriatric dog can have his nutritional needs met, as can puppies and growing dogs. The calorie content of these foods is adjusted accordingly. With the correct amount of the right foods and the proper amount of exercise, your Pekingese should stay in top shape. Again, common sense must prevail. Too many calories will increase weight, too few will reduce weight.

Occasionally, a young Pekingese going through the teething period will become a poor eater. The concerned owner's first response is to tempt the dog by hand-feeding special treats and foods that the problem eater seems to prefer. This practice only serves to compound the problem. Once the dog learns to play the waiting game, he will turn up his nose at anything other than his favorite food, knowing full well that what he *wants* to eat will eventually arrive.

Unlike humans, dogs have no suicidal tendencies. A healthy dog will not starve himself to death. He may not eat enough to keep him in the shape we find ideal and attractive, but he will definitely eat enough to maintain himself. If your Pekingese is not eating properly and appears to be too thin, it is probably best to consult your veterinarian.

## SPECIAL NEEDS OF THE PEKINGESE

### Hot Weather

Caution must be exercised in hot weather. First of all, the Pekingese is not a breed that particularly enjoys being exposed to hot summer sun, nor can short-nosed breeds like the Peke tolerate high temperatures. Heat stroke is

*Due to their heavy coats, it is important to protect your Pekingese from exposure to high temperatures for prolonged periods of time.*

*This Pekingese has the right idea; on a warm day there is nothing like a quick dip in the pool!*

not uncommon. Plan your Peke's outings for the first thing in the morning if possible. If you cannot arrange to do this, wait until the sun has set and the outdoor temperature has dropped to a comfortable degree.

You must *never* leave your Pekingese in a car in hot weather, even for a few minutes. Temperatures can soar rapidly, and your dog can die of heat exhaustion in less time than you would ever imagine. Rolling down the windows helps little and is dangerous in that an overheated Pekingese will panic and could attempt to escape through the open window. A word to the wise—leave your dog at home in a cool room on hot days.

On the other hand, cold weather does not bother most Pekes. Ours love the snow. Do not allow your Pekingese to remain wet if the two of you get caught in the rain, however. At the very least, you should towel dry the wet Pekingese. Better still, use your blow dryer (set on medium) to make sure your dog is thoroughly dry and mat free as indicated in the chapter on bathing and grooming.

*This relaxed Pekingese enjoys a cool breeze while lounging in the summer sun.*

If coat upkeep gets to be too much of a chore, a trim might be the way to go. A trimmed-down Peke is cute as can be, and if you live in a warm climate and just have a pet, it probably would be much cooler for the dog and easier for you to take care of the coat.

We always have ice packs—the kind that are used to keep food cold in coolers—for the dogs to lie on in very hot weather. They are wonderful for traveling and in places where there might not be any air conditioning.

## Eye Care

The Peke's most outstanding feature is his large lustrous eyes. The eyes, however, are also extremely susceptible to damage because they are so prominent. Ulceration can take place very quickly from something as simple as dust blown about on a windy day. Of course, injuries can occur in day-to-day play with another dog, or when the Peke is foraging around in tall grass or weeds.

Inverted eyelids (entropion) can also be a cause of eye irritation and subsequent ulceration. It is important to check your Peke's eyes at every grooming session and seek a veterinarian's advice the minute you see any blue haze on the eyeball. Even the tiniest pinpoint of discoloration can lead to problems, so be safe rather than sorry.

*The Pekingese is an active and energetic dog that will benefit greatly from plenty of playtime.*

## Special Handling

It is important that everyone in the family knows how to properly pick up a Pekingese. Never pick up a Peke by his front legs, as it is easy to dislocate the shoulders or seriously injure a leg. The Peke should be lifted with one hand under the dog's chest, just behind the front legs. The other hand should support the dog's rear.

Never place a Peke on a couch or chair. Jumping from high places (for a Peke!) can cause serious injuries to the back. Pekes can be prone to back injuries, so it is best to avoid their having to manipulate stairs or jumping down out of automobiles.

## Exercise

If your own exercise proclivities lie closer to a walk around the block than to ten-mile marathon runs, your choice of a Pekingese was probably a wise one. The Pekingese is not a breed that requires taking your energy level to its outer limits. In fact, the Pekingese self-exercise if they are allowed the freedom to do so. If your Pekingese shares his life with children or another Peke, he will undoubtedly be getting all the exercise he needs to stay fit. A Pekingese is always ready for a romp or even to invent some new game that entails plenty of aerobic activity.

This does not mean that your Pekingese will not benefit from a short daily walk down the block. On the contrary, slow, steady exercise in weather that is not too hot will do nothing but extend your Peke's life. If your Pekingese is doing all this with you at his side, you are increasing the chances that the two of you will enjoy each other's company for many more years to come.

Naturally, common sense must be used in the extent and intensity of the exercise you give your Pekingese. A fast walk for you can be full-tilt for your Pekingese. Remember that young puppies have short bursts of energy and then require long rest periods. No puppy of any breed should be forced to accompany you on extended walks. Serious injuries can result. Again—short exercise periods and long rest stops for any Pekingese under 10 or 12 months of age.

## Socialization

The Pekingese is, by nature, a happy dog and takes most situations in stride. It is important to accommodate the breed's natural instincts by making sure your dog is accustomed to everyday events of all kinds. Traffic, strange noises, loud or hyperactive children, and strange animals can be very intimidating to a dog of any breed that has never experienced them before. Gently and gradually, introduce your puppy to as many strange situations as you possibly can.

Make it a practice to take your Pekingese with you everywhere, whenever practical. The breed is a real crowd-pleaser, and you will find your Pekingese will savor all the attention he gets.

*Pekingese are very social creatures and need the company of others—this trio takes a play break on the lawn.*

## COMMON SENSE

A dog cannot talk and tell you if there is something wrong, so it is up to you to use common sense and avoid your Peke getting into problem areas. Pekes are very courageous and will try things that might not be appropriate for their conformation and size. Be careful.

*The Pekingese puppy is no stranger to mischief—always carefully supervise your little fellow when outdoors.*

*The Pekingese is by nature a happy dog that makes friends easily—this group will be pals for a lifetime!*

Get to know your veterinarian and rely upon that professional to advise you if ever you have any questions regarding your Pekingese. An experienced vet undoubtedly knows what you may only be able to guess at.

# GROOMING Your Pekingese

## REGULAR COAT CARE

Much of what initially attracts people to the Pekingese is his beautiful coat. We wish we could tell you that it does not take much to maintain that look. Unfortunately, we can't. Your Pekingese will only have that special look as long as you are diligent in keeping his coat thoroughly groomed. You must either learn to do this yourself or find a reliable groomer.

This cannot be accomplished by occasional attacks on the problem after long

*This little Pekingese gets ready to enjoy his favorite activity after grooming—a mud bath!*

*It may be hard work to achieve the Pekingese's meticulously groomed look, but remember, a well-groomed dog is a healthy dog, and a healthy dog is a happy dog!* periods of neglect. The damage done by neglecting the Pekingese coat can normally only be undone by shaving away the dog's entire coat because of the mats that have developed. This is neither attractive nor is it good for your dog. If you are not willing to put in the time and effort necessary to maintain the Pekingese coat, which to a great extent constitutes a good part of the breed's essence, why not get a smooth-coated dog instead? It is not necessary to maintain the *length* of coat the Pekingese needs for the show ring, but maintaining the correct look of the breed is important.

## Puppy Coat

Undoubtedly, the breeder from whom you purchased your Pekingese will have begun to accustom the puppy to grooming as soon as there was enough hair to brush. You must continue with the grooming sessions or begin them at once if for some

reason they have not been started. You and your Pekingese
will spend many hours involved with this activity over a
lifetime, so it is imperative that you both learn to cooperate in
the endeavor to make it an easy and pleasant experience.

The first piece of equipment you should obtain is a
grooming table. This can be built or purchased at your local
pet emporium. Even a sturdy snack table topped with a non-
skid pad can be used, just so long as it is steady and does not
wobble or shake. An unsteady table is a very frightening thing
for any dog.

Make sure that whatever kind of table you use is of a height
at which you can sit or stand and work comfortably.
Adjustable-height grooming tables are available at most pet
shops.

You will also need to invest in a good brush, a steel comb,
barber's scissors, and a pair of nail clippers. Unless you keep
your dog's coat extremely short, an electric hair dryer with
heat control is a
must. Electric
clippers can be
useful as well. We

*In order to achieve the Pekingese's well-
groomed appearance, you will need to
acquire the appropriate grooming tools.*

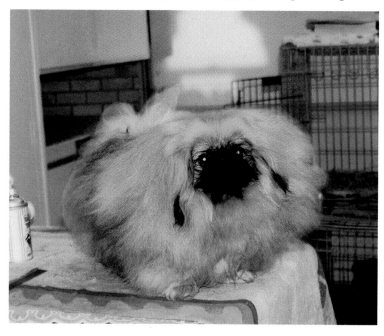

will discuss their value a little further along. Also very useful is a good-quality, spray-type coat conditioner. Consider the fact that you will be using these grooming tools for many years to come, so buy the best of these items that you can afford.

The brush that you will need is called a pin brush (sometimes called a Poodle brush). The pin brush, along with the fine-toothed comb, nail clippers, and coat conditioner, can be purchased at your local pet shop or at any dog show.

Do not attempt to groom your puppy on the floor. He will only attempt to get away from you when he has decided that enough is enough, and you will spend a good part of your time chasing the puppy around the room. Nor is sitting on the floor for long stretches of time the most comfortable position in the world for the average adult.

*Before bathing your Pekingese, you must brush his coat thoroughly to be sure it is mat free.*

The Pekingese puppy should be taught to lie down and on his side to be groomed. You will find the bit of effort you invested in teaching the puppy to lie on his side will be time well spent, as it will permit you to work on the harder-to-reach areas.

Begin this training by laying the puppy down on his side on the table. Speak reassuringly to the puppy, stroking his head and rump. (This is a good time to practice the stay command.) Do this a number of times before you attempt to do any grooming. Repeat the process until your puppy understands what he is supposed to do when you place him on the grooming table.

Fortunately (or unfortunately, however you see it) a Peke's puppy coat is the most difficult to deal with. When the coat matures, it will be hair rather than fluff. To brush the puppy coat, start with the pin brush.

Begin with your puppy lying on his side. You will begin what is called "line brushing" at the top of the shoulder. Part the hair in a straight line from the front of the shoulder straight on down to the bottom of the chest. Brush through the hair to the right and left of the part. Mist the part with an anti-static spray or conditioner. Start at the skin and brush out to the very end of the hair. Do a small section at a time and continue down the part. When you reach the bottom of the part, return to the top and make another part just to the right of the first line you brushed. *Part, brush, and mist.* You will repeat this process, moving each part toward the rear until you reach the puppy's tail.

*This little show prospect has been brushed and trimmed and is now ready for her turn in the ring.*

I prefer to do the legs on the same side I have been working on at this time. Use the same process, parting the hair at the top of the leg and working down. Do this all around the leg and be especially careful to attend to the hard-to-reach areas under the upper legs where they join the body. Mats occur in these areas very rapidly.

Should you encounter a mat that does not brush out easily, use your fingers and the steel comb to help separate the hairs as much as possible. Do not cut or pull out the matted hair. Apply coat conditioner directly to the mat and brush completely from the skin out.

When you have finished the legs on the one side, turn the puppy over and complete the entire process on the other side—*part, brush, and spray.* As your Pekingese becomes accustomed to this process, you may find the puppy considers this naptime. You may have to lift your puppy into the standing position to arouse him from his slumber.

With the puppy standing, do the chest and tail. When brushing, do so gently so as not to break the hair. When brushing on and around the rear legs, make sure to give special attention to the area of the anus and genitalia. Needless to say, it is important to be extremely careful when brushing in these areas in that they are very sensitive and easily injured.

Use your fine-toothed comb around the head and ears, being very careful not to poke the eye.

## Nail Trimming

This is a good time to accustom your Pekingese to having his nails trimmed and his feet inspected. Always inspect your dog's feet for cracked pads. If your Pekingese is allowed out in the yard or accompanies you to the park or woods, check between the toes for splinters and thorns. Pay particular attention to any swollen or tender areas. In many sections of the country, there is a weed called a foxtail that releases a small, barbed, hook-like affair that carries its seed. This hook easily finds its way into a dog's foot or between his toes and very quickly works its way deep into the dog's flesh. This will rapidly cause soreness and infection. These barbs should be removed by your veterinarian before serious problems result.

Many Pekes spend most of their lives indoors or on grass when outdoors, which permits the nails to grow long very quickly. Do not allow the nails to become overgrown and then expect to cut them back easily. Each nail has a blood vessel running through the center called the quick. The quick grows close to the end of the nail and contains very sensitive nerve endings. If the nail is allowed to grow too long, it will be impossible to cut it back to a proper length without cutting into the quick. This causes severe pain to the dog and can also result in a great deal of bleeding that can be very difficult to stop.

Should the quick be nipped in the trimming process, there are any number of blood clotting products available at pet shops that will almost immediately stem the flow of blood. It is wise to have one of these products on hand in case there is a nail trimming accident or the dog tears a nail on his own.

## Grooming the Adult Pekingese

Ideally you and your Pekingese have spent the many months

between puppyhood and full maturity learning to assist each other through the grooming process. The

*If you accustom your Pekingese to grooming procedures at an early age, he will come to think of it as a pleasant experience.*

*You must never ignore your Pekingese's feet during grooming. Check for cracked footpads and keep his nails trimmed short to prevent injury.*

two of you have survived the changing of the puppy coat and the arrival of the entirely different adult hair. The hair of the adult Pekingese is profuse but of a texture that is far less apt to mat.

The method of brushing the adult coat is the same as that used since your Pekingese was a puppy. The only real difference is that you have a bit more dog and the hair itself will be longer unless you cut it back.

While one might expect grooming an adult Pekingese to be a monumental task, this is not necessarily so. The important thing is consistency. A few minutes a day, every day, precludes your dog's hair from becoming a tangled mess that may take you hours to undo. Then too, the two of you have been practicing the brushing routine for so long it has undoubtedly become second nature to both of you.

Some owners take great pride in keeping the coat of their Pekingese very full. This, of course, is an absolute requirement if you wish to show your Pekingese. Most pet owners, however, find this an extremely demanding task and keep the coat cut back to a moderate length. Scissors can be used to cut the coat back to a manageable length, and the electric clippers can be used to remove the hair from the frequently matted "arm pits," under the legs where they join the body, and under the dog's stomach.

If you do not care to keep the coat long, a Pekingese can be kept in a very cute "puppy trim." The body is clipped with electric clippers using a No. 4 blade. The ears and tail are left longer to maintain the distinctive Pekingese look.

Hair should be removed from between the toe pads. You can use barber scissors or electric clippers to accomplish this.

## BATHING

Bathe the dog once a week, or whenever needed. Use a quality shampoo made especially for dogs. A Pekingese should never be bathed until after he has been thoroughly brushed. If all mats are not out before you bathe, you will end up with a fused cotton ball! Mats will only get worse when doused with water.

A small cotton ball placed inside each ear will prevent water from running down into the dog's ear canal, and a drop or two of mineral oil or a dab of petroleum jelly placed around the rim of each eye will preclude shampoo irritation.

A rubber mat should be placed at the bottom of the tub so that your dog does not slip and become frightened. A rubber spray hose is necessary to remove all shampoo residue. Rinse thoroughly, apply a quality coat conditioner, and rinse again.

In bathing, start behind the ears and work back. Finally, wash around the face, being very careful not to get suds into your Peke's sensitive eyes. Rinse well. Shampoo residue in the coat is sure to dry the hair and could cause skin irritation.

As soon as you have completed the bath, use a heavy towel to remove as much of the excess water as possible. Your

*This lovely Pekingese obviously enjoys showing off her good grooming for the camera!*

Pekingese will undoubtedly assist you in the process by shaking a great deal of the water out of the coat on his own.

## Using a Hair Dryer

*Take special care when cleaning your Peke's delicate ears—wipe them gently with cleanser and a moist cloth.*

It is very important to gently brush dry your Pekingese using your pin brush and a hair dryer. Always set the hair dryer at the medium setting, never hot. The hot setting may be quicker, but it will also dry out the hair and could easily burn the delicate skin of your Pekingese.

*Never allow your Pekingese to remain wet after a bath. Wrap him in a clean towel and dry him thoroughly.*

Keep the ears clean by putting in a little ear cleanser and wiping with a tissue. Do not probe into the ear beyond where you can see! The delicate eardrum can be easily injured. If you suspect a problem further down in the ear canal, consult your veterinarian.

# HOUSEBREAKING and Training Your Pekingese

There is no breed of dog that cannot be trained. It does appear some breeds are more difficult to get the desired response from than others are. In many cases, however, this has more to do with the trainer and his or her training methods than with the dog's inability to learn. With the proper approach, any dog that is not mentally deficient can be taught to be a good canine citizen. Many dog owners do not understand how a dog learns, nor do they realize they can be breed specific in their approach to training.

Young puppies have an amazing capacity to learn. This capacity is greater than most humans realize. It is important to remember though, these young puppies also easily forget unless they are reminded of what they have learned by continual reinforcement.

As puppies leave the nest, they begin their search for two things: a pack leader, and the rules set down by that leader by which the puppies can abide. Because puppies, particularly Pekingese puppies, are cuddly, cute, and very small, their owners fail miserably in supplying these very basic needs of every dog. Instead, the owner immediately begins to respond to the demands of the puppy.

For example, a puppy quickly learns that he will be allowed into the house or a room because he is barking or whining, not because he can only enter the house when he is *not* barking or whining. Instead of learning that the only way he will be fed is to follow a set procedure (i.e., sitting or lying down on command), he learns that leaping about the kitchen or barking incessantly is what gets results.

If the young puppy cannot find his pack leader in an owner, the puppy assumes the role of pack leader. Yes, even as small as that bit of fluff is, if there are no rules imposed, the Pekingese puppy learns to make his own rules. Unfortunately, the negligent owner continually reinforces the puppy's decisions by allowing him to govern the household.

With small dogs like our Pekingese, this scenario can produce a neurotic nuisance. In large dogs, the situation can be downright dangerous. Neither situation is an acceptable one.

The key to successful training lies in establishing the proper relationship between dog and owner. The owner, or the owning family, must be the pack leader, and the individual or family must provide the rules by which the dog abides.

*Crates make housetraining your pet much easier because dogs do not want to soil where they eat and sleep.*

Once this is established, ease of training depends in great part upon just how much a dog depends upon his master's approval. The entirely dependent dog lives to please his master and will do everything in his power to evoke the approval response from the person to whom he is devoted.

At the opposite end of the pole, we have the totally independent dog that is not remotely concerned with what his master thinks or wants. Dependency varies from one breed to the next, and, to a degree, within breeds as well. Pekingese are no exception to this rule. As we have already said, the Pekingese can and does have a mind of his own–some more than others. At times, your patience will be tested.

## HOUSEBREAKING

### The Crate Method

*Avoidance* is a major key to successfully training your Pekingese, whether it is obedience training or housebreaking. It is much easier for your Pekingese to learn something if you do not first have to have him unlearn some bad habit. Crate training is a highly successful method of avoiding bad habits before they begin.

First-time dog owners are inclined to initially see the crate or cage method of housebreaking as cruel, but those same people will return later and thank us profusely for having suggested it in the first place. They are also surprised to find that the puppy will eventually come to think of his crate as a place of private retreat—a den to which he will go for rest and privacy. The

*Bonding is by far one of the most important building blocks of training. This little Pekingese revels in the love and attention he gets from his owner.*

success of the crate method is based upon the fact that puppies will not soil the area in which they sleep unless they are forced to.

Use of a cage reduces house training time to an absolute minimum and avoids keeping a puppy under constant stress by incessantly correcting him for making mistakes in the house. The anti-cage advocates consider it cruel to confine a puppy for any length of time, but find no problem in constantly harassing and punishing the puppy because he has wet on the carpet or relieved himself behind the sofa.

Crates come in a wide variety of styles. The fiberglass shipping kennels used by most airlines are popular with many Pekingese owners, but residents of the extremely warm climates sometimes prefer the wire cage type. Both are available at pet stores.

The crate used for housebreaking should only be large enough for the puppy to stand, lie down, and stretch out comfortably. There are many sizes to choose from. We advise using either the No. 100 or 200 size airline-type crate. These sizes seem ideal for most Pekingese.

Begin to feed your Pekingese puppy in his crate. Keep the

door closed and latched while the puppy is eating. When the meal is finished, open the cage and *carry* the

*Housebreaking your Pekingese relies on your patient and consistent reinforcement.*

*Look at those sad puppy eyes! Be sure to offer your Pekingese plenty of positive reinforcement and in no time at all, he'll be obeying every command.*

puppy outdoors to the spot where you want him to learn to eliminate. In the event you do not have outdoor access, or will be away from home for long periods of time, begin housebreaking by placing newspapers in some out-of-the-way corner that is easily accessible for the puppy. If you consistently take your puppy to the same spot, you will reinforce the habit of going there for that purpose.

It is important that you do not let the puppy loose after eating. Young puppies will eliminate almost immediately after eating or drinking. They will also be ready to relieve themselves when they first wake up and after playing. If you keep a watchful eye on your puppy, you will quickly learn when this is about to take place. A puppy usually circles and sniffs the floor just before he relieves himself. Because the Peke is so close to the ground, you must pay very close attention to what your puppy is doing. Do not give your puppy an opportunity to learn that he can eliminate in the house! Your house training chores will be reduced considerably if you avoid this happening in the first place.

*Very basic training can begin at a relatively early age, once a puppy has been vaccinated and housebroken.*

If you are not able to watch your puppy every minute, he should be in his crate with the door securely latched. Each time you put your puppy in the crate, give him a small treat of some kind. Throw the treat to the back of the crate and encourage the puppy to walk in on his own. When he does so, praise the puppy and perhaps hand him another piece of the treat through the opening in the front of the crate.

Do not succumb to your puppy's complaints about being in his crate. The puppy must learn to stay there and to do so without unnecessary complaining. A quick no command and a tap on the crate will usually get the puppy to understand that theatrics will not result in liberation. (Remember, as the pack leader, you make the rules and the puppy is seeking to learn what they are!)

Do understand a puppy of 8 to 12 weeks will not be able to contain himself for long periods. Puppies of that age must relieve themselves every few hours, except at night. Your schedule must be adjusted accordingly. Also, make sure that your puppy has relieved himself—both bowel and bladder—the last thing at night and do not dawdle when you wake up in the morning.

Your first priority in the morning is to get the puppy outdoors. Just how early this ritual takes place will depend much more upon your puppy than upon you. If your Pekingese is like most others, there will be no doubt in your mind when he needs to be let out. You will also very quickly learn to tell the difference between the "this is an emergency" complaint and the "I just want out" grumbling. Do not test the young puppy's ability to contain himself. His vocal demand to be let out is confirmation that the housebreaking lesson is being learned.

### Home Alone

Should you find it necessary to be away all day and your puppy is home alone, you will not be able to leave the pup in a crate. On the other hand, do not make the mistake of allowing him to roam the house, or even a large room, at will. Confine the puppy to a very small room or partitioned area and cover the floor with newspaper. Make this area large enough so that the puppy will not have to relieve himself next to his bed, food, or water bowl. You will soon find that the puppy will be inclined to use one particular spot to perform his bowel and bladder functions. When you are home, you must take the puppy to this exact spot to eliminate at the appropriate time.

### BASIC TRAINING

Where you are emotionally and the environment in which you train are just as important to your dog's training as is his

*Training your Pekingese will be easier once he is accustomed to wearing a leash.*

state of mind at the time. Never begin training when you are irritated, distressed, or preoccupied. Nor should you begin basic training in a place that interferes with you or your dog's concentration. At first, the two of you should work in a place where you can concentrate fully upon each other. Once the commands are understood and learned, you can begin testing your dog in public places.

*A young puppy will not know the difference between good and bad behavior. It is up to you, the owner, to teach him what is acceptable in your household.*

You must be aware of the sensitivity level of your Pekingese, his independent nature, and his love of fun and games. Pekingese respond well to lots of praise and activities that they believe are fun games. They do not respond to yelling or being struck. Never resort to shaking or striking your Pekingese puppy. A very stern "no!" is usually more than sufficient, and even with the most persistent unwanted behavior, striking the ground with a rolled up newspaper is about as extreme as you will ever need to be.

We cannot say that the Peke takes to obedience training like a duck to water, but at the same time, some owners have persisted and wound up with little dogs that have surprised us all with their ability. Much depends upon the individual Peke.

### The No Command

There is no doubt whatsoever that one of the most important commands your Pekingese puppy will ever learn is the meaning of the no command. It is critical that the puppy learns this command as soon as possible. One important piece of advice in using this and all other commands—*never give a command you are not prepared and able to enforce!* A good leader does not enforce rules arbitrarily. The only way a puppy learns to obey commands is to realize that once issued, commands must be complied with. Learning the no command should start on the first day of the puppy's arrival at your home.

Be fair to your dog. He can easily learn the difference between things he can and cannot do. A dog is unable to learn that there are some things he can do one time but not the next. Yelling at your dog for lying on the bed today when it was perfectly all right for him to do so the previous day serves only to confuse.

## Leash Training

Begin leash training by putting a soft, lightweight collar on your puppy. After a few hours of occasional scratching at the unaccustomed addition, your puppy will quickly forget it is even there.

It may not be necessary for the puppy or adult Pekingese to wear his collar and identification tags within the confines of your home later, but no Pekingese should ever leave home without a collar and the attached leash held securely in your hand.

Begin getting your puppy accustomed to his collar by leaving it on for a few minutes at a time. Gradually extend the time you leave the collar on. Once this is accomplished, attach a lightweight leash to the collar while you are playing with the puppy. At first, do not try to guide the puppy. You are only trying to get the puppy used to having something attached to his collar.

Get your puppy to follow you as you move around by coaxing him along with a treat of some kind. Let the puppy smell what you have in your hand, then move a few steps back, holding the treat in front of his nose. As soon as the puppy takes a few steps toward you, praise him enthusiastically and continue to do so as you continue to move along.

Make the first few lessons brief and fun for the puppy. Continue the lessons in your home or yard

*Although your puppy will want to learn what you have to teach him, keep in mind that his attention span is short and he will need plenty of repetition and praise.*

*Don't let life pass your Pekingese by! Proper training will allow him to participate in all the excitement life has to offer.* until the puppy is completely unconcerned about the fact that he is on a leash. With a treat in one hand and the leash in the other, you can begin to use both to guide the puppy in the direction you wish to go. Eventually, the two of you can venture out on the sidewalk in front of your house and then on to adventures everywhere! This is one lesson no puppy is too young to learn.

## The Come Command

The next most important lesson for the Pekingese puppy to learn is to come when called. This is one lesson that you *must* associate with fun, games, and treats. It is an important one, but one your Peke will have great difficulty responding to if he sees anything at all negative in the exercise.

It is very important that the puppy learn his name as soon as possible. Constant repetition is what does the trick in teaching a puppy his name. Use the name every time you talk to your puppy. Talk to your dog? There is a quotation we particularly like that appeared in an old British dog book we found regarding conversations with our canine friends. It simply states: "Of course you should talk to your dogs. But talk sense!"

Learning to come on command could save your dog's life when the two of you venture out into the world. Come is the command a dog must understand has to be obeyed without question, but remember that your Peke should not associate the command with fear. Your dog's response to his name and the word come should always be associated with a pleasant experience, such as great praise and petting, and perhaps a treat of his favorite snack.

*Basic obedience training is necessary for your dog, not only to teach him acceptable behavior, but to keep him safe as well.*

Again, remember that it is much easier to avoid the establishment of bad habits than it is to correct them once set. *Never* give the come command unless you are sure your puppy will come to you.

The very young puppy is far more inclined to respond to the come command than the older dog. Young Peke puppies are far more dependent upon you. An older Peke may well lose a good part of that dependency and become preoccupied with his surroundings. So, start your come on command training early on.

Use the command initially when the puppy is already on his way to you, or give the command while walking or running away from the youngster. Clap your hands and sound very happy and excited about having the puppy join in on this "game."

The very young Pekingese puppy will normally want to stay as close to his owner as possible, especially in strange surroundings. When your puppy sees you moving away, his natural inclination will be to get close to you. This is a perfect time to use the come command.

*There are basic training commands that every dog should know how to perform. This Pekingese is learning the sit-stay command.*

You may want to attach a long leash or light rope to the puppy's collar to ensure the correct response. Never chase or punish your puppy for not obeying the come command. Doing so in the initial stages of training makes the youngster associate the command with something to fear, and this will result in avoidance rather than the immediate positive response you desire. It is imperative that you praise your Pekingese puppy and give him a treat when he does come to you, even if he voluntarily delays his response for many minutes.

### The Sit and Stay Commands

Just as important to your Pekingese puppy's safety as the no command and learning to come when called are the sit and stay commands. Even very young Pekingese can learn the sit command quickly, especially if it appears to be a game and a food treat is involved.

First, remember that the Pekingese-in-training should always be on a collar and leash for all of his lessons. A Pekingese puppy is curious about everything, but he can become bored with anything that goes on too long. A puppy is not beyond getting up and walking away when he has decided he needs to investigate something.

Give the sit command just before you reach down and exert pressure on your puppy's rear. Praise the puppy profusely when he does sit, although it was you who exerted the effort. A food treat of some kind always seems to make the experience more enjoyable for the puppy.

Continue holding the dog's rear end down and repeat the sit command several times. If your puppy attempts to get up, repeat the command yet again while exerting pressure on the rear end until the correct position is assumed. Make your puppy stay in this position a little bit longer with each succeeding lesson. Begin with a few seconds and increase the time as the lessons progress over the following weeks.

If your puppy attempts to get up or to lie down, he should be corrected by simply saying, "sit," in a firm voice. This should be accompanied by returning the dog to the desired position. Only when *you* decide your dog may get up should he be allowed to do so. Do not test the extent of your young Pekingese puppy's patience. Remember that you are dealing with a baby and the attention span of any youngster is relatively limited. When you do decide the dog can get up, call his name, say, "OK," and make a big fuss over him. Praise and a food treat are in order every time your Pekingese responds correctly.

Once your puppy has mastered the sit lesson, you may start on the stay command. With your Pekingese on leash and facing you, command him to sit, then take a step or two back. If your dog attempts to get up to follow, firmly say, "sit, stay!" While you are saying this, raise your hand, palm toward the dog, and again command, "stay!"

If your dog attempts to get up, you must correct him at once, returning him to the sit position and repeating, "stay!" Once your Pekingese begins to understand what you want, you can gradually increase the distance in which you step back. With a long leash attached to your dog's collar, start with a few steps and gradually increase the distance to several yards. It is important for your Pekingese to learn that the sit, stay command must be obeyed no matter how far away you are. With advanced training, your Pekingese can be taught that the command is to be obeyed even when you leave the room or are entirely out of sight.

As your Pekingese becomes accustomed to responding to this lesson and is able to remain in the sit position for as long as you command, do not end the command by calling the dog to you. Walk back to your Pekingese and say, "OK." This will let your dog know the command is over. When your Pekingese becomes entirely dependable in this lesson, you can then call the dog to you.

The sit, stay command can take considerable time and patience to get across to puppies. You must not forget that their attention span will be short. Keep the stay part of the lesson very short until your puppy is about six months old.

## The Down Command

Do not try to teach your Pekingese puppy too many things at once. Wait until you have mastered one lesson before moving on to something new.

When you feel quite confident that your puppy is comfortable with the sit and stay commands, you can start work on down. This is the single word command for lie down. Use the

*This little party-goer demonstrates the ultimate in good behavior. If it wasn't for basic training, that birthday cake would surely be devoured!*

down command *only* when you want the dog to lie down. If you want your Pekingese to get off your sofa or to stop jumping up on people, use the off command. Do not interchange these two commands. Doing so will only serve to confuse your dog, and evoking the right response will become next to impossible.

The down position is especially useful if you want your Pekingese to remain in one place for a long period. Most dogs are far more inclined to stay put when lying down than when they are sitting or standing.

*If you are patient and consistent when training your puppy, you'll have a well-behaved adult Pekingese as a reward.*

Teaching this command to your Pekingese may take more time and patience than the previous lessons the two of you have undertaken. It is believed by some animal behaviorists that assuming the down position somehow represents greater submissiveness.

With your Pekingese sitting in front of and facing you, hold a treat in your right hand with the excess part of the leash in your left. Hold the treat under the dog's nose and slowly bring your hand down to the ground. Your dog will follow the treat with his head and neck. As he does, give the down command and exert *light* pressure on the dog's shoulders with your left. If your dog resists the pressure on his shoulders, *do not continue pushing down*. Doing so will only create more resistance. Reach down and slide the dog's feet toward you until he is lying down.

An alternative method of getting your Pekingese headed into the down position is to move around to the dog's right side and, as you draw his attention downward with your right hand, place your left hand under the dog's front legs and gently slide them forward. You will undoubtedly have to be on your knees next to the youngster in order to do this.

As your dog's forelegs begin to slide out to his front, keep moving the treat along until the dog's whole body is lying on the ground while you continually repeat, "down." Once your dog has assumed the position you desire, give him the treat and a lot of praise. Continue assisting your Pekingese into the down position until he does so on his own. Be firm and be patient.

## The Heel Command

In learning to heel, your Pekingese will walk on your left side with his shoulder next to your leg, no matter which direction you might go or how quickly you turn. Learning this command can be an extremely valuable lesson for your dog, even though he is a Toy breed. A Pekingese that darts back and forth in front of or under his master's feet can endanger himself and cause serious injury for his owner as well.

Teaching your Pekingese to heel is critical to off-leash control and will not only make your daily walks more enjoyable, it will make a far more tractable companion when the two of you are in crowded or confusing situations. We do not recommend ever allowing your Pekingese to be off leash when you are away from home, but it is important to know that you can control your dog no matter what the circumstances are.

A lightweight, rounded leather collar or a small jeweler's snake chain are best for training long-haired Toy dogs, especially for the heeling lesson. Changing from the collar your dog regularly wears to something different indicates that what you are doing is business and not just a casual stroll. The pet shop at which you purchase your other supplies can assist you in selecting the best training collar that will help with your lessons but not catch in your dog's hair.

As you train your Pekingese puppy to walk along on the leash, you should accustom the youngster to walk on your left side. The leash should cross your body from the dog's collar to your right hand. The excess portion of the leash will be folded into your right hand and your left hand on the leash will be used to make corrections.

A quick, gentle jerk on the leash with your left hand will keep your dog

*The time you invest in training your Pekingese will benefit the both of you for a lifetime. These two Pekingese buddies make up a beautiful wreath of holiday cheer.*

*Pekingese are naturally mischievous and playful. Basic training will be much more successful if you make it fun and interesting.*

from lunging side to side, pulling ahead, or darting between your legs. As you make a correction, give the heel command. Keep the leash loose when your dog maintains the proper position at your side.

If your dog begins to drift away, give the leash a quick jerk and guide the dog back to the correct position and give the heel command. Do not pull on the lead with steady pressure. What is needed is a sharp but gentle jerking motion to get your dog's attention.

### VERSATILITY

There is no end to the number of activities you and your Pekingese can enjoy together. The breed is highly successful in conformation shows and some do well in obedience trials.

Owners not inclined toward competitive events might find enjoyment in having their Pekingese serve as therapy dogs. Dogs used in this area are trained to bring comfort to the sick, the elderly, and often the handicapped. You would be amazed at the sparkle of delight that a jolly Peke brings to the eyes of those who are confined to a bed or wheelchair.

Some Pekingese have proven themselves to be of outstanding assistance to the hearing impaired. Pekes can signal their owners to the sound of the phone, the doorbell, or of someone knocking or calling. This can be a wonderful addition to someone's life.

The well-trained Pekingese can provide a whole world of activities for the owner. You are limited only by the amount of time you wish to invest in this remarkable breed.

# SPORT of Purebred Dogs

Welcome to the exciting and sometimes frustrating sport of dogs. No doubt you are trying to learn more about dogs or you wouldn't be deep into this book. This section covers the basics that may entice you, further your knowledge and help you to understand the dog world.

Dog showing has been a very popular sport for a long time and has been taken quite seriously by some. Others only enjoy it as a hobby.

The Kennel Club in England was formed in 1859, the American Kennel Club was established in 1884 and the Canadian Kennel Club was formed in 1888. The purpose of these clubs was to register purebred dogs and maintain their Stud Books. In the beginning, the concept of registering dogs was not readily accepted. More than 36 million dogs have been enrolled in the AKC Stud Book since its inception in 1888. Presently the kennel clubs not only register dogs but

*Shown as part of the Toy Group at AKC-sanctioned shows, many Pekingese enjoy successful careers in the show ring. Ch. St. Aubrey Dragonora Of Elsdon, owned by Anne E. Snelling.*

adopt and enforce rules and regulations governing dog shows, obedience trials and field trials. Over the years they have fostered and encouraged interest in the health and welfare of the purebred dog. They routinely donate funds to veterinary research for study on genetic disorders.

Below are the addresses of the kennel clubs in the United States, Great Britain and Canada.

The American Kennel Club
51 Madison Avenue
New York, NY 10010
(Their registry is located at: 5580 Centerview Drive, STE 200, Raleigh, NC 27606-3390)

The Kennel Club
1 Clarges Street
Piccadilly, London, WIY 8AB, England

The Canadian Kennel Club
111 Eglinton Avenue
East Toronto, Ontario M6S 4V7
Canada

*This Pekingese poses with one of the many Chinese artworks that seem to depict his ancestors.*

Today, there are numerous activities that are enjoyable for both the dog and the handler. Some of the activities include conformation showing, obedience competition, tracking, agility, the Canine Good Citizen Certificate, and a wide range of instinct tests that vary from breed to breed. Where you start depends upon your goals which early on may not be readily apparent.

## Puppy Kindergarten

Every puppy will benefit from this class. PKT is the foundation for all future dog activities from conformation to "couch potatoes." Pet owners should make an effort to attend even if they never expect to show their dog. The class is designed for puppies about three months of age with graduation at approximately five months of age. All the puppies will be in the same age group and, even though some may be a little unruly, there should not be any real problem.

This class will teach the puppy some beginning obedience. As in all obedience classes the owner learns how to train his own dog. The PKT class gives the puppy the opportunity to interact with other puppies in the same age group and exposes him to strangers, which is very important. Some dogs grow up with behavior problems, one of them being fear of strangers. As you can see, there can be much to gain from this class.

There are some basic obedience exercises that every dog should learn. Some of these can be started with puppy kindergarten.

## Sit

One way of teaching the sit is to have your dog on your left side with the leash in your right hand, close to the collar. Pull up on the leash and at the same time reach around his hindlegs with your left hand and tuck them in. As you are doing this say, "Beau, sit." Always use the dog's name when you give an active command. Some owners like to use a treat holding it over the dog's head. The dog will need to sit to get the treat. Encourage the dog to hold the sit for a few seconds, which will eventually be the beginning of the Sit/Stay. Depending on how cooperative he is, you can rub him under the chin or stroke his back. It is a good time to establish eye contact.

## Down

Sit the dog on your left side and kneel down beside him with the leash in your right hand. Reach over him with your left hand and grasp his left foreleg. With your right hand, take his right foreleg and pull his legs forward while you say, "Beau, down." If he tries to get up, lean on his shoulder to encourage him to stay down. It will relax your dog if you stroke his back while he is down. Try to encourage him to stay down for a few seconds as preparation for the Down/Stay.

## Heel

The definition of heeling is the dog walking under control at your left heel. Your puppy will learn controlled walking in the puppy kindergarten class, which will eventually lead to heeling. The command is "Beau, heel," and you start off briskly with your left foot. Your leash is in your right hand and your left hand is holding it about half way down. Your left hand should be able to control the leash and there should be a little slack in it. You want him to walk with you with your leg somewhere between his nose and his shoulder. You need to encourage him to stay with you, not forging (in front of you) or lagging behind you. It is best to keep him on a fairly short lead. Do not allow the lead to become tight. It is far better to give him a little jerk when necessary and remind him to heel. When you come to a halt, be prepared physically to make him sit. It takes practice to become coordinated. There are excellent books on training that you may wish to purchase. Your instructor should be able to recommend one for you.

*Group training classes are not only a good way to teach basic obedience commands, they also allow invaluable opportunities for socialization.*

### Recall

This quite possibly is the most important exercise you will ever teach. It should be a pleasant experience. The puppy may learn to do random recalls while being attached to a long line such as a clothes line. Later the exercise will start with the dog sitting and staying until called. The command is "Beau, come." Let your command be happy. You want your dog to come willingly and faithfully. The recall could save his life if he sneaks out the door. In practicing the recall, let him jump on you or touch you before you reach for him. If he is shy, then kneel down to his level. Reaching for the insecure dog could frighten him, and he may not be willing to come again in the future. Lots of praise and a treat would be in order whenever you do a recall. Under no circumstances should you ever correct your dog when he has come to you. Later in formal obedience your dog will be required to sit in front of you after recalling and then go to heel position.

### CONFORMATION

Conformation showing is our oldest dog show sport. This type of showing is based on the dog's appearance—that is his structure, movement and attitude. When considering this type of showing, you need to be aware of your breed's standard and be able to evaluate your dog compared to that standard. The breeder of your puppy or other experienced breeders would be good sources for such an evaluation. Puppies can go through lots of changes over a period of time. Many puppies start out as promising hopefuls and then after maturing may be disappointing as show candidates. Even so this should not deter them from being excellent pets.

Usually conformation training classes are offered by the local kennel or obedience clubs. These are excellent places for training puppies. The puppy should be able to walk on a lead before entering such a class. Proper ring procedure and technique for posing (stacking) the dog will be demonstrated as well as gaiting the dog. Usually certain patterns are used in the ring such as the triangle or the "L." Conformation class, like the PKT class, will give your youngster the opportunity to socialize with different breeds of dogs and humans too.

It takes some time to learn the routine of conformation showing. Usually, one starts at the puppy matches that may be AKC Sanctioned or Fun Matches. These matches are generally for puppies from two or three months to a year old, and there may be classes for the adult over the age of 12 months. Similar to point shows, the classes are divided by sex and after completion of the classes in that breed or variety, the class winners compete for Best of Breed or Variety. The winner goes on to compete in the Group and the Group winners compete for Best in Match. No championship points are awarded for match wins.

A few matches can be great training for puppies even though there is no intention to go on showing. Matches enable the puppy to meet new people and be handled by a stranger— the judge. It is also a change of environment, which broadens the horizon for both dog and handler. Matches and other dog activities boost the confidence of the handler and especially the younger handlers.

Earning an AKC championship is built on a point system, which is different from Great Britain. To become an AKC Champion of Record the dog must earn 15 points. The number of points earned each time depends upon the number of dogs in competition. The number of points available at each show depends upon the breed, its sex and the location of the show. The United States is divided into ten AKC zones. Each zone has its own set of points. The purpose of the zones is to try to equalize the points available from breed to breed and area to area.The AKC adjusts the point scale annually.

The number of points that can be won at a show are between one and five. Three-, four- and five-point wins are considered majors. Not only does the dog need 15 points won under three different judges, but those points must include two majors under two different judges. Canada also works on a point system but majors are not required.

Dogs always show before bitches. The classes available to those seeking points are: Puppy (which may be divided into 6 to 9 months and 9 to 12 months); 12 to 18 months; Novice; Bred-by-Exhibitor; American-bred; and Open. The class winners of the same sex of each breed or variety compete against each other for Winners Dog and Winners Bitch. A Reserve Winners Dog and Reserve Winners Bitch are also awarded but do not carry any points unless the Winners win is disallowed by AKC. The Winners Dog and Bitch

*In conformation, your dog is judged by how closely he conforms to the breed standard.*

compete with the specials (those dogs that have attained championship) for Best of Breed or Variety, Best of Winners and Best of Opposite Sex. It is possible to pick up an extra point or even a major if the points are higher for the defeated winner than those of Best of Winners. The latter would get the higher total from the defeated winner.

At an all-breed show, each Best of Breed or Variety winner will go on to his respective Group and then the Group winners will compete against each other for Best in Show. There are seven Groups: Sporting, Hounds, Working, Terriers, Toys, Non-Sporting and Herding. Obviously there are no Groups at speciality shows (those shows that have only one breed or a show such as the American Spaniel Club's Flushing Spaniel Show, which is for all flushing spaniel breeds).

Earning a championship in England is somewhat different since they do not have a point system. Challenge Certificates are awarded if the judge feels the dog is deserving regardless of the number of dogs in competition. A dog must earn three Challenge Certificates under three different judges, with at least one of these Certificates being won after the age of 12 months. Competition is very strong and entries may be higher than they are in the US. The Kennel Club's Challenge Certificates are only available at Championship Shows.

In England, The Kennel Club regulations require that certain dogs, Border Collies and Gundog breeds, qualify in a working capacity (i.e., obedience or field trials) before becoming a full Champion. If they do not qualify in the working aspect, then

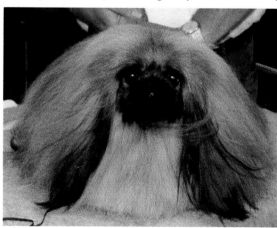

*Good grooming is essential to a Pekingese's success in the show ring.*

they are designated a Show Champion, which is equivalent to the AKC's Champion of Record. A Gundog may be granted the title of Field Trial Champion (FT Ch.) if he passes all the tests in the field but would also have to qualify in conformation before becoming a full Champion. A Border Collie that earns the title of Obedience Champion (Ob Ch.) must also qualify in the conformation ring before becoming a Champion.

*If your Pekingese is destined for life in the show ring, part of his basic training must prepare him for handling by judges.*

The US doesn't have a designation full Champion but does award for Dual and Triple Champions. The Dual Champion must be a Champion of Record, and either Champion Tracker, Herding Champion, Obedience Trial Champion or Field Champion. Any dog that has been awarded the titles of Champion of Record, and any two of the following: Champion Tracker, Herding Champion, Obedience Trial Champion or Field Champion, may be designated as a Triple Champion.

The shows in England seem to put more emphasis on breeder judges than those in the US There is much competition within the breeds. Therefore the quality of the individual breeds should be very good. In the United States we tend to have more "all around judges" (those that judge multiple breeds) and use the breeder judges at the specialty shows. Breeder judges are more familiar with their own breed since they are actively breeding that breed or did so at one time. Americans emphasize Group and Best in Show wins and promote them accordingly.

The shows in England can be very large and extend over several days, with the Groups being scheduled on different days. Though multi-day shows are not common in the US, there are cluster shows, where several different clubs will use the same show site over consecutive days.

Westminster Kennel Club is our most prestigious show although the entry is limited to 2,500. In recent years, entry has been limited to Champions. This show is more formal than the majority of the shows with the judges wearing formal attire and the handlers fashionably dressed. In most instances the quality of the dogs is superb. After all, it is a show of Champions. It is a good show to study the AKC registered breeds and is by far the most exciting—especially since it is televised! WKC is one of the few shows in this country that is still benched. This means the dog must be in his benched area during the show hours except when he is being groomed, in the ring, or being exercised.

Typically, the handlers are very particular about their appearances. They are careful not to wear something that will detract from their dog but will perhaps enhance it. American ring procedure is quite formal compared to that of other countries. There is a certain etiquette expected between the judge and exhibitor and among the other exhibitors. Of course it is not always the case but the judge is supposed to be polite, not engaging in small talk or acknowledging how well he knows the handler. There is a more informal and relaxed atmosphere at the shows in other countries. For instance, the dress code is more casual. I can see where this might be more fun for the exhibitor and especially for the novice. The US is very handler-oriented in many of the breeds. It is true, in most

*POPpups™ are healthy treats for your Pekingese. When bone-hard they help to control plaque build-up; when microwaved they become a rich cracker which your Peke will love. The POPpup™ is available in liver and other flavors and is fortified with calcium.*

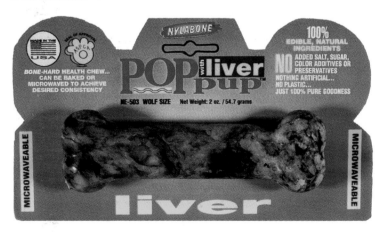

*The 1994 Westminster Group winner, Ch. Briarcourt's Damien Gable, owned by Nancy H. Shapland and bred and handled by David Fitzpatrick.*

instances, that the experienced professional handler can present the dog better and will have a feel for what a judge likes.

In England, Crufts is The Kennel Club's own show and is most assuredly the largest dog show in the world. They've been known to have an entry of nearly 20,000, and the show lasts four days. Entry is only gained by qualifying through winning in specified classes at another Championship Show. Westminster is strictly conformation, but Crufts exhibitors and spectators enjoy not only conformation but obedience, agility and a multitude of exhibitions as well. Obedience was admitted in 1957 and agility in 1983.

If you are handling your own dog, please give some consideration to your apparel. For sure the dress code at matches is more informal than the point shows. However, you should wear something a little more appropriate than beach attire or ragged jeans and bare feet. If you check out the handlers and see what is presently fashionable, you'll catch on. Men usually dress with a shirt and tie and a nice sports coat. Whether you are male or female, you will want to wear comfortable clothes and shoes. You need to be able to run with your dog and you certainly don't want to take a chance of falling and hurting yourself. Heaven forbid, if nothing else, you'll upset your dog. Women usually wear a dress or two-piece outfit, preferably with pockets to carry bait, comb, brush, etc. In this case men are the lucky ones with all their pockets. Ladies, think about where your dress will be if you need to kneel on the floor and also think about running. Does it allow freedom to do so?

You need to take along dog; crate; ex pen (if you use one); extra newspaper; water pail and water; all required grooming equipment, including hair dryer and extension cord; table; chair for you; bait for dog and lunch for you and friends; and, last but not least, clean up materials, such as plastic bags, paper towels, and perhaps a bath towel and some shampoo—just in case. Don't forget your entry confirmation and directions to the show.

If you are showing in obedience, then you will want to wear pants. Many of our top obedience handlers wear pants that are color-coordinated with their dogs. The philosophy is that imperfections in the black dog will be less obvious next to your black pants.

Whether you are showing in conformation, Junior Showmanship or obedience, you need to watch the clock and be sure you are not late. It is customary to pick up your conformation armband a few minutes before the start of the class. They will not wait for you and if you are on the show grounds and not in the ring, you will upset everyone. It's a little more complicated picking up your obedience armband if you show later in the class. If you have not picked up your armband and they get to your number, you may not be allowed to show. It's best to pick up your armband early, but then you may show earlier than expected if other handlers don't pick up. Customarily all conflicts should be discussed with the judge prior to the start of the class.

## Junior Showmanship

The Junior Showmanship Class is a wonderful way to build self confidence even if there are no aspirations of staying with the dog-show game later in life. Frequently, Junior Showmanship becomes the background of those who become successful exhibitors/handlers in the future. In some instances it is taken very seriously, and success is measured in terms of wins. The Junior Handler is judged solely on his ability and skill in presenting his dog. The dog's conformation is not to be considered by the judge. Even so the condition and grooming of the dog may be a reflection upon the handler.

Usually the matches and point shows include different classes. The Junior Handler's dog may be entered in a breed or obedience class and even shown by another person in that class. Junior Showmanship classes are usually divided by age and perhaps sex. The age is determined by the handler's age on the day of the show. The classes are:

*Handlers must pose their Pekingese in the most flattering position to emphasize the dog's specific strengths.*

**Novice Junior** for those at least ten and under 14 years of age who at time of entry closing have not won three first places in a Novice Class at a licensed or member show.

**Novice Senior** for those at least 14 and under 18 years of age who at the time of entry closing have not won three first places in a Novice Class at a licensed or member show.

**Open Junior** for those at least ten and under 14 years of age who at the time of entry closing have won at least three first places in a Novice Junior Showmanship Class at a licensed or member show with competition present.

**Open Senior** for those at least 14 and under 18 years of age who at time of entry closing have won at least three first places in a Novice Junior Showmanship Class at a licensed or member show with competition present.

Junior Handlers must include their AKC Junior Handler number on each show entry. This needs to be obtained from the AKC.

## Canine Good Citizen

The AKC sponsors a program to encourage dog owners to train their dogs. Local clubs perform the pass/fail tests, and dogs who pass are awarded a Canine Good Citizen Certificate. Proof of vaccination is required at the time of participation. The test includes:

1. Accepting a friendly stranger.
2. Sitting politely for petting.
3. Appearance and grooming.
4. Walking on a loose leash.
5. Walking through a crowd.
6. Sit and down on command/staying in place.
7. Come when called.
8. Reaction to another dog.
9. Reactions to distractions.
10. Supervised separation.

If more effort was made by pet owners to accomplish these exercises, fewer dogs would be cast off to the humane shelter.

*Canine good citizens must be able to get along well with other animals. This group of friends look as if they've passed the test.*

*Is it any wonder that this Pekingese is behaving? Surely he thinks all of those presents are for him!*

## OBEDIENCE

Obedience is necessary, without a doubt, but it can also become a wonderful hobby or even an obsession. Obedience classes and competition can provide wonderful companionship, not only with your dog but with your classmates or fellow competitors. It is always gratifying to discuss your dog's problems with others who have had similar experiences. The AKC acknowledged Obedience around 1936, and it has changed tremendously even though many of the exercises are basically the same. Today, obedience competition is just that—very competitive. Even so, it is possible for every obedience exhibitor to come home a winner (by earning qualifying scores) even though he/she may not earn a placement in the class.

Most of the obedience titles are awarded after earning three qualifying scores (legs) in the appropriate class under three different judges. These classes offer a perfect score of 200, which is extremely rare. Each of the class exercises has its own point value. A leg is earned after receiving a score of at least 170 and at least 50 percent of the points available in each exercise. The titles are:

## Companion Dog–CD
This is called the Novice Class and the exercises are:

| | |
|---|---|
| 1. Heel on leash and figure 8 | 40 points |
| 2. Stand for examination | 30 points |
| 3. Heel free | 40 points |
| 4. Recall | 30 points |
| 5. Long sit–one minute | 30 points |
| 6. Long down–three minutes | 30 points |
| Maximum total score | 200 points |

## Companion Dog Excellent–CDX
This is the Open Class and the exercises are:

| | |
|---|---|
| 1. Heel off leash and figure 8 | 40 points |
| 2. Drop on recall | 30 points |
| 3. Retrieve on flat | 20 points |
| 4. Retrieve over high jump | 30 points |
| 5. Broad jump | 20 points |
| 6. Long sit–three minutes (out of sight) | 30 points |
| 7. Long down–five minutes (out of sight) | 30 points |
| Maximum total score | 200 points |

## Utility Dog–UD
The Utility Class exercises are:

| | |
|---|---|
| 1. Signal Exercise | 40 points |
| 2. Scent discrimination-Article 1 | 30 points |
| 3. Scent discrimination-Article 2 | 30 points |
| 4. Directed retrieve | 30 points |
| 5. Moving stand and examination | 30 points |
| 6. Directed jumping | 40 points |
| Maximum total score | 200 points |

After achieving the UD title, you may feel inclined to go after the UDX and/or OTCh. The UDX (Utility Dog Excellent) title went into effect in January 1994. It is not easily attained. The title requires qualifying simultaneously ten times in Open B and Utility B but not necessarily at consecutive shows.

The OTCh (Obedience Trial Champion) is awarded after the dog has earned his UD and then goes on to earn 100 championship points, a first place in Utility, a first place in Open and another first place in either class. The placements must be won under three different judges at all-breed obedience trials. The points are determined by the number of dogs competing in the Open B and Utility B classes. The OTCh title precedes the dog's name.

Obedience matches (AKC Sanctioned, Fun, and Show and Go) are usually available. Usually they are sponsored by the local obedience clubs. When preparing an obedience dog for a title, you will find matches very helpful. Fun Matches and Show and Go Matches are more lenient in allowing you to make corrections in the ring. This type of training is usually very necessary for the Open and Utility Classes. AKC Sanctioned Obedience Matches do not allow corrections in the ring since they must abide by the AKC Obedience Regulations. If you are interested in showing in obedience, then you should contact the AKC for a copy of the Obedience Regulations.

## AGILITY

Agility was first introduced by John Varley in England at the Crufts Dog Show, February 1978, but Peter Meanwell, competitor and judge, actually developed the idea. It was officially recognized in the early '80s. Agility is extremely popular in England

*Every Pekingese is a champion in his owner's eyes and this little guy is sure of it!*

103

and Canada and growing in popularity in the US. The AKC acknowledged agility in August 1994. Dogs must be at least 12 months of age to be entered. It is a fascinating sport that the dog, handler, and spectators enjoy to the utmost. Agility is a spectator sport! The dog performs off lead. The handler either runs with his dog or positions himself on the course and directs his dog with verbal and hand signals over a timed course over or through a variety of obstacles including a time out or pause. One of the main drawbacks to agility is finding a place to train. The obstacles take up a lot of space and it is very time consuming to put up and take down courses.

The titles earned at AKC agility trials are Novice Agility Dog (NAD), Open Agility Dog (OAD), Agility Dog Excellent (ADX), and Master Agility Excellent (MAX). In order to acquire an agility title, a dog must earn a qualifying score in its respective class on three separate occasions under two different judges. The MAX will be awarded after earning ten qualifying scores in the Agility Excellent Class.

### PERFORMANCE TESTS

During the last decade the American Kennel Club has promoted performance tests—those events that test the different breeds' natural abilities. This type of event encourages a handler to devote even more time to his dog and retain the natural instincts of his breed heritage. It is an important part of the wonderful world of dogs.

### GENERAL INFORMATION

Obedience, tracking and agility allow the purebred dog with an Indefinite Listing Privilege (ILP) number or a limited

*There are so many activities that you and your dog can participate in and the versatile Pekingese has the ability to excel at them all.*

registration to be exhibited and earn titles. Application must be made to the AKC for an ILP number.

The American Kennel Club publishes a monthly *Events* magazine that is part of the *Gazette*, their official journal for the sport of purebred dogs. The *Events* section lists upcoming shows and the secretary or superintendent for them. The majority of the conformation shows in the US are overseen by licensed superintendents. Generally the entry closing date is approximately two-and-a-half weeks before the actual show. Point shows are fairly expensive, while the match shows cost about one third of the point show entry fee. Match shows usually take entries the day of the show but some are pre-entry. The best way to find match show information is through your local kennel club. Upon asking, the AKC can provide you with a list of superintendents, and you can write and ask to be put on their mailing lists.

Obedience trial and tracking test information is available through the AKC. Frequently these events are not superintended, but put on by the host club. Therefore you would make the entry with the event's secretary.

*A healthy and tasty treat for your Pekingese because they love cheese is CHOOZ. CHOOZ are bone-hard but can be microwaved to expand into a huge, crispy dog biscuit. They are almost fat free and about 70 percent protein.*

As you have read, there are numerous activities you can share with your dog. Regardless what you do, it does take teamwork. Your dog can only benefit from your attention and training. We hope this chapter has enlightened you and hope, if nothing else, you will attend a show here and there. Perhaps you will start with a puppy kindergarten class, and who knows where it may lead!

# HEALTH CARE

Veterinary medicine has become far more sophisticated than what was available to our ancestors. This can be attributed to the increase in household pets and consequently the demand for better care for them. Also human medicine has become far more complex. Today diagnostic testing in veterinary medicine parallels human diagnostics. Because of better technology we can expect our pets to live healthier lives thereby increasing their life spans.

*Laboratory tests are studied by highly trained veterinary technicians. Most tests are performed right in your own veterinarian's office.*

### THE FIRST CHECK UP

You will want to take your new puppy/dog in for his first check up within 48 to 72 hours after acquiring him. Many breeders strongly recommend this check up and so do the humane shelters. A puppy/dog can appear healthy but he may have a serious problem that is not apparent to the layman. Most pets have some type of a minor flaw that may never cause a real problem.

Unfortunately if he/she should have a serious problem, you will want to consider the consequences of keeping the pet and the attachments that will be formed, which may be broken prematurely. Keep in mind there are many healthy dogs looking for good homes.

This first check up is a good time to establish yourself with the veterinarian and learn the office policy regarding their

*Breeding dogs of only the best quality ensures that good health and temperament is passed down to each generation. This mom teaches her youngster how to unpack the grocery bags.*

hours and how they handle emergencies. Usually the breeder or another conscientious pet owner is a good reference for locating a capable veterinarian. You should be aware that not all veterinarians give the same quality of service. Please do not make your selection on the least expensive clinic, as they may be short changing your pet. There is the possibility that eventually it will cost you more due to improper diagnosis, treatment, etc. If you are selecting a new veterinarian, feel free to ask for a tour of the clinic. You should inquire about making an appointment for a tour since all clinics are working clinics, and therefore may not be available all day for sightseers. You may worry less if you see where your pet will be spending the day if he ever needs to be hospitalized.

## THE PHYSICAL EXAM

Your veterinarian will check your pet's overall condition, which includes listening to the heart; checking the respiration; feeling the abdomen, muscles and joints; checking the mouth, which includes the gum color and signs of gum disease along with plaque buildup; checking the ears for signs of an infection or ear mites; examining the eyes; and, last but not least, checking the condition of the skin and coat.

He should ask you questions regarding your pet's eating and elimination habits and invite you to relay your questions. It is a good idea to prepare a list so as not to forget anything. He should discuss the proper diet and the quantity to be fed. If this should differ from your breeder's recommendation, then you should convey to him the breeder's choice and see if he approves. If he recommends changing the diet, then this should be done over a few days so as not to cause a gastrointestinal upset. It is customary to take in a fresh stool sample (just a small amount) for a test for intestinal parasites. It must be fresh, preferably within 12 hours, since the eggs hatch quickly and after hatching will not be observed under the microscope. If your pet isn't obliging then, usually the technician can take one in the clinic.

## IMMUNIZATIONS

It is important that you take your puppy/dog's vaccination record with you on your first visit. In case of a puppy, presumably the breeder has seen to the vaccinations up to the time you acquired custody. Veterinarians differ in their vaccination protocol. It is not unusual for your puppy to have

*There are all kinds of flying disks for dogs, but only one is made with strength, scent, and originality. The Nylabone® Frisbee™\* is a must if you want to have this sort of fun with your Pekingese.*
\*The trademark Frisbee is used under license from Mattel, Inc., California, USA

received vaccinations for distemper, hepatitis, leptospirosis, parvovirus, and parainfluenza every two to three weeks from the age of five or six weeks. Usually this is a combined injection and is typically called the DHLPP. The DHLPP is given through at least 12 to 14 weeks of age, and it is customary to continue with another parvovirus vaccine at 16 to 18 weeks.

*The Pekingese puppy should be energetic and alert. Any changes in his activity should be brought to your veterinarian's attention immediately.*

*Regular medical care is extremely important throughout your Pekingese's life. Vaccination boosters and physical exams are part of your dog's lifelong maintenance.*

You may wonder why so many immunizations are necessary. No one knows for sure when the puppy's maternal antibodies are gone, although it is customarily accepted that distemper

antibodies are gone by 12 weeks. Usually parvovirus antibodies are gone by 16 to 18 weeks of age. However, it is possible for the maternal antibodies to be gone at a much earlier age or even a later age. Therefore immunizations are started at an early age. The vaccine will not give immunity as long as there are maternal antibodies.

The rabies vaccination is given at three or six months of age depending on your local laws. A vaccine for bordetella (kennel cough) is advisable and can be given anytime from the age of five weeks. The coronavirus is not commonly given unless there is a problem locally. The Lyme vaccine is necessary in endemic areas. Lyme disease has been reported in 47 states.

## Distemper

This is virtually an incurable disease. If the dog recovers, he is subject to severe nervous disorders. The virus attacks every tissue in the body and resembles a bad cold with a fever. It can cause a runny nose and eyes and cause gastrointestinal disorders, including a poor appetite, vomiting and diarrhea. The virus is carried by raccoons, foxes, wolves, mink and other dogs. Unvaccinated youngsters and senior citizens are very susceptible. This is still a common disease.

## Hepatitis

This is a virus that is most serious in very young dogs. It is spread by contact with an infected animal or its stool or urine. The virus affects the liver and kidneys and is characterized by high fever, depression and lack of appetite. Recovered animals may be afflicted with chronic illnesses.

## Leptospirosis

This is a bacterial disease transmitted by contact with the urine of an infected dog, rat or other wildlife. It produces severe symptoms of fever, depression, jaundice and internal bleeding and was fatal before the vaccine was developed. Recovered dogs can be carriers, and the disease can be transmitted from dogs to humans.

## Parvovirus

This was first noted in the late 1970s and is still a fatal disease. However, with proper vaccinations, early diagnosis and prompt treatment, it is a manageable disease. It attacks the bone marrow and intestinal tract. The symptoms include depression, loss of appetite, vomiting, diarrhea and collapse. Immediate medical attention is of the essence.

## Rabies
This is shed in the saliva and is carried by raccoons, skunks, foxes, other dogs and cats. It attacks nerve tissue, resulting in paralysis and death. Rabies can be transmitted to people and is virtually always fatal. This disease is reappearing in the suburbs.

*Bordetella attached to canine cilia. Otherwise known as kennel cough, this disease is highly contagious and should be vaccinated against routinely.*

## Bordetella (Kennel Cough)
The symptoms are coughing, sneezing, hacking and retching accompanied by nasal discharge usually lasting from a few days to several weeks. There are several disease-producing organisms responsible for this disease. The present vaccines are helpful but do not protect for all the strains. It usually is not life threatening but in some instances it can progress to a serious bronchopneumonia. The disease is highly contagious. The vaccination should be given routinely for dogs that come in contact with other dogs, such as through boarding, training class or visits to the groomer.

## Coronavirus
This is usually self limiting and not life threatening. It was first noted in the late '70s about a year before parvovirus. The virus produces a yellow/brown stool and there may be depression, vomiting and diarrhea.

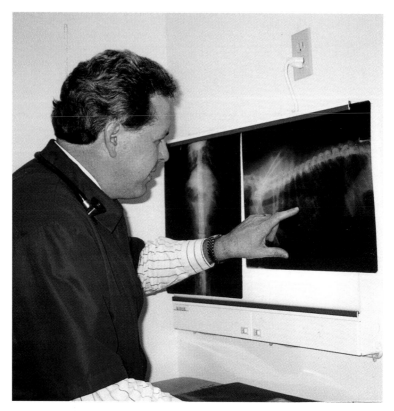

*Regular visits to the veterinarian will help in the timely diagnosis of any illnesses or parasitic infections.*

Lyme Disease

This was first diagnosed in the United States in 1976 in Lyme, CT in people who lived in close proximity to the deer tick. Symptoms may include acute lameness, fever, swelling of joints, and loss of appetite. Your veterinarian can advise you if you live in an endemic area.

After your puppy has completed his puppy vaccinations, you will continue to booster the DHLPP once a year. It is customary to booster the rabies one year after the first vaccine and then, depending on where you live, it should be boostered every year or every three years. This depends on your local laws. The Lyme and corona vaccines are boostered annually and it is recommended that the bordetella be boostered every six to eight months.

## Annual Visit

I would like to impress the importance of the annual check up, which would include the booster vaccinations, check for intestinal parasites and test for heartworm. Today in our very busy world it is rush, rush and see "how much you can get for how little." Unbelievably, some non-veterinary businesses have entered into the vaccination business. More harm than good can come to your dog through improper vaccinations, possibly from inferior vaccines and/or the wrong schedule. More than likely you truly care about your companion dog and over the years you have devoted much time and expense to his well being. Perhaps you are unaware that a vaccination is not just a vaccination. There is more involved. Please, please follow through with regular physical examinations. It is so important for your veterinarian to know your dog and this is especially true during middle age through the geriatric years. More than likely your older dog will require more than one physical a year. The annual physical is good preventive medicine. Through early diagnosis and subsequent treatment your dog can maintain a longer and better quality of life.

*The deer tick is the most common carrier of Lyme disease. Photo courtesy of Virbac Laboratories, Inc., Fort Worth, Texas.*

## Intestinal Parasites

### Hookworms

These are almost microscopic intestinal worms that can cause anemia and therefore serious problems, including death, in young puppies. Hookworms can be transmitted to humans through penetration of the skin. Puppies may be born with them.

### Roundworms

These are spaghetti-like worms that can cause a potbellied appearance and dull coat along with more severe symptoms, such as vomiting, diarrhea, and coughing. Puppies acquire these while in the mother's uterus and through lactation. Both hookworms and roundworms may be acquired through ingestion.

## Whipworms

These have a three-month life cycle and are not acquired through the dam. They cause intermittent diarrhea usually with mucus. Whipworms are possibly the most difficult worm to eradicate. Their eggs are very resistant to most environmental factors and can last for years until the proper conditions enable them to mature. Whipworms are seldom seen in the stool.

Intestinal parasites are more prevalent in some areas than others. Climate, soil and contamination are big factors contributing to the incidence of intestinal parasites. Eggs are passed in the stool, lay on the ground and then become infective in a certain number of days. Each of the above worms has a different life cycle. Your best chance of becoming and remaining worm-free is to always pooper-scoop your yard. A fenced-in yard keeps stray dogs out, which is certainly helpful.

I would recommend having a fecal examination on your dog twice a year or more often if there is a problem. If your dog has a positive fecal sample, then he will be given the appropriate medication and you will be asked to bring back another stool sample in a certain period of time (depending on the type of worm) and then be rewormed. This process goes on until he has at least two negative samples. The different types of worms require different medications. You will be wasting your money and doing your dog an injustice by buying over-the-counter medication without first consulting your veterinarian.

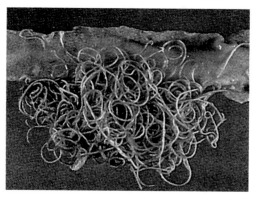

*When visiting the veterinarian, it is customary to take a stool sample to test for intestinal parasites, such as roundworms. Courtesy of Merck AgVet.*

## Coccidiosis and Giardiasis

These protozoal infections usually affect puppies, especially in places where large numbers of puppies are brought together. Older dogs may harbor these infections but do not show signs unless they are stressed. Symptoms include diarrhea, weight loss and lack of appetite. These infections are not always apparent in the fecal examination.

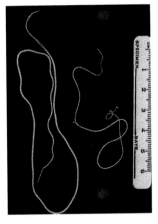

*Whipworms are hard to detect, and it is a job best left to a veterinarian. Pictured here are adult whipworms.*

*Tapeworms are long, flat, ribbon-like segmented parasites that often grow to several feet in length.*

## Tapeworms

Seldom apparent on fecal floatation, they are diagnosed frequently as rice-like segments around the dog's anus and the

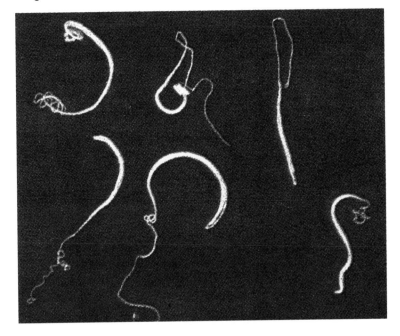

base of the tail. Tapeworms are long, flat and ribbon like, sometimes several feet in length, and made up of many segments about five-eighths of an inch long. The two most common types of tapeworms found in the dog are:

(1)  First the larval form of the flea tapeworm parasite must mature in an intermediate host, the flea, before it can become infective. Your dog acquires this by ingesting the flea through licking and chewing.

(2)  Rabbits, rodents and certain large game animals serve as intermediate hosts for other species of tapeworms. If your dog should eat one of these infected hosts, then he can acquire tapeworms.

### HEARTWORM DISEASE

This is a worm that resides in the heart and adjacent blood vessels of the lung that produces microfilaria, which circulate in the bloodstream. It is possible for a dog to be infected with any number of worms from one to a hundred that can be 6 to 14 inches long. It is a life-threatening disease, expensive to treat and easily prevented. Depending on where you live, your veterinarian may recommend a preventive year-round and either an annual or semiannual blood test. The most common preventive is given once a month.

### EXTERNAL PARASITES

### Fleas

These pests are not only the dog's worst enemy but also enemy to the owner's pocketbook. Preventing is less expensive than treating, but regardless we'd prefer to spend our money elsewhere. Likely, the majority of our dogs are allergic to the bite of a flea, and

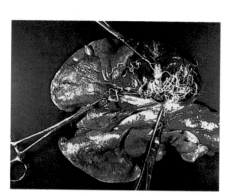

*Dirofilaria—adult worms in the heart of a dog. Courtesy of Merck AgVet.*

116

*The cat flea is the most common flea of both dogs and cats. Courtesy of Fleabusters, RX for Fleas Inc., Fort Lauderdale, Florida.*

in many cases it only takes one flea bite. The protein in the flea's saliva is the culprit. Allergic dogs have a reaction, which usually results in a "hot spot." More than likely such a reaction will involve a trip to the veterinarian for treatment. Yes, prevention is less expensive. Fortunately today there are several good products available.

If there is a flea infestation, no one product is going to correct the problem. Not only will the dog require treatment so will the environment. In general flea collars are not very effective although there is now available an "egg" collar that will kill the eggs on the dog. Dips are the most economical but they are messy. There are some effective shampoos and treatments available through pet shops and veterinarians. An oral tablet arrived on the American market in 1995 and was popular in Europe the previous year. It sterilizes the female flea but will not kill adult fleas. Therefore the tablet, which is given monthly, will decrease the flea population but is not a "cure-all." Those dogs that suffer from flea-bite allergy will still be subjected to the bite of the flea. Another popular parasiticide is permethrin, which is applied to the back of the dog in one or two places depending on the dog's weight. This product works as a repellent causing the flea to get "hot feet" and jump off. Do not confuse this product with some of the organophosphates that are also applied to the dog's back.

Some products are not usable on young puppies. Treating fleas should be done under your veterinarian's guidance. Frequently it is necessary to combine products and the layman does not have the knowledge regarding possible toxicities. It is hard to believe but there are a few dogs that do have a natural resistance to fleas. Nevertheless it would be wise to treat all pets at the same time. Don't forget your cats. Cats just love to prowl the neighborhood and consequently return with unwanted guests.

Adult fleas live on the dog but their eggs drop off the dog into the environment. There they go through four larval stages before reaching adulthood, and thereby are able to jump back on the poor unsuspecting dog. The cycle resumes and takes between 21 to 28 days under ideal conditions. There are environmental products available that will kill both the adult fleas and the larvae.

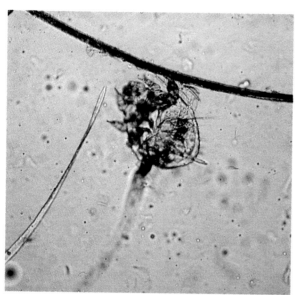

*Sarcoptic mange is highly contagious to other dogs as well as humans. Sarcoptes cause intense itching.*

## Ticks

Ticks carry Rocky Mountain Spotted Fever, Lyme disease and can cause tick paralysis. They should be removed with tweezers, trying to pull out the head. The jaws carry disease. There is a tick preventive collar that does an excellent job. The ticks automatically back out on those dogs wearing collars.

## Sarcoptic Mange

This is a mite that is difficult to find on skin scrapings. The pinnal reflex is a good indicator of this disease. Rub the ends of the pinna (ear) together and

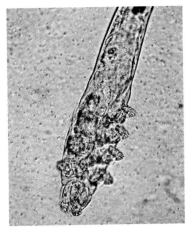

*Demodectic mange is passed from a dam to her puppies. It involves areas of hair loss.*

the dog will start scratching with his foot. Sarcoptes are highly contagious to other dogs and to humans although they do not live long on humans. They cause intense itching.

## Demodectic Mange

This is a mite that is passed from the dam to her puppies. It affects youngsters age three to ten months. Diagnosis is confirmed by skin scraping. Small areas of alopecia around the eyes, lips and/or forelegs become visible. There is little itching unless there is a secondary bacterial infection. Some breeds are afflicted more than others.

## Cheyletiella

This causes intense itching and is diagnosed by skin scraping. It lives in the outer layers of the skin of dogs, cats, rabbits and humans. Yellow-gray scales may be found on the back and the rump, top of the head and the nose.

## To Breed or Not To Breed

More than likely your breeder has requested that you have your puppy neutered or spayed. Your breeder's request is based on what is healthiest for your dog and what is most beneficial for your breed. Experienced and conscientious breeders devote many years into developing a bloodline. In order to do this, he makes every effort to plan each breeding in regard to conformation, temperament and health. This type of breeder does his best to perform the necessary testing (i.e., OFA, CERF, testing for inherited blood disorders, thyroid, etc.). Testing is expensive and sometimes very disheartening when a favorite dog doesn't pass his health tests. The health history pertains not only to the breeding stock but to the immediate ancestors. Reputable breeders do not want their offspring to be bred indiscriminately. Therefore you may be asked to neuter or spay your puppy. Of course there is always the exception, and your breeder may agree to let you breed your dog under his direct supervision. This is an important concept. More and more effort is being made to breed healthier dogs.

*For the sake of your puppy as well as the health of your family, you should bring your new Pekingese to the veterinarian within three days of his arrival at your home.*

## Spay/Neuter

There are numerous benefits of performing this surgery at six months of age. Unspayed females are subject to mammary and ovarian cancer. In order to prevent mammary cancer she must be spayed prior to her first heat cycle. Later in life, an unspayed female may develop a pyometra (an infected uterus), which is definitely life threatening.

*The Hercules™ is made of very tough polyurethane. It is designed for Pekingese who like to chew. The raised dental tips massage the gums and remove the plaque they encounter during chewing.*

Spaying is performed under a general anesthetic and is easy on the young dog. As you might expect it is a little harder on the older dog, but that is no reason to deny her the surgery. The surgery removes the ovaries and uterus. It is important to remove all the ovarian tissue. If some is left behind, she could remain attractive to males. In order to view the ovaries, a reasonably long incision is necessary. An ovariohysterectomy is considered major surgery.

Neutering the male at a young age will inhibit some characteristic male behavior that owners frown upon. Some boys will not hike their legs and mark territory if they are neutered at six months of age. Also neutering at a young age has hormonal benefits, lessening the chance of hormonal aggressiveness.

Surgery involves removing the testicles but leaving the scrotum. If there should be a retained testicle, then he definitely needs to be neutered before the age of two or three years. Retained testicles can develop into cancer. Unneutered males are at risk for testicular cancer, perineal fistulas, perianal tumors and fistulas and prostatic disease.

Intact males and females are prone to housebreaking accidents. Females urinate

*All Pekingese are cute, but not all are of breeding quality. Reputable breeders will often sell pet-quality dogs on the condition that they are spayed or neutered.*

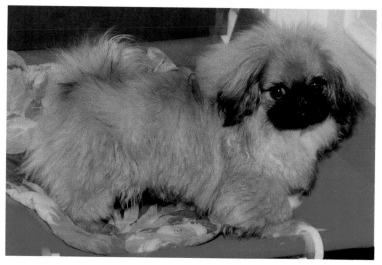

*Spaying/neutering is often the best option for your family pet. The health benefits are numerous and it will minimize the risk of certain diseases.* frequently before, during and after heat cycles, and males tend to mark territory if there is a female in heat. Males may show the same behavior if there is a visiting dog or guests.

Surgery involves a sterile operating procedure equivalent to human surgery. The incision site is shaved, surgically scrubbed and draped. The veterinarian wears a sterile surgical gown, cap, mask and gloves. Anesthesia should be monitored by a registered technician. It is customary for the veterinarian to recommend a pre-anesthetic blood screening, looking for metabolic problems and a ECG rhythm strip to check for normal heart function. Today anesthetics are equal to human anesthetics, which enables your dog to walk out of the clinic the same day as surgery.

Some folks worry about their dog gaining weight after being neutered or spayed. This is usually not the case. It is true that some dogs may be less active so they could develop a problem, but most dogs are just as active as they were before surgery. However, if your dog should begin to gain, then you need to decrease his food and see to it that he gets a little more exercise.

# DENTAL CARE for Your Dog's Life

So you've got a new puppy! You also have a new set of puppy teeth in your household. Anyone who has ever raised a puppy is abundantly aware of these new teeth. Your puppy will chew anything it can reach, chase your shoelaces, and play "tear the rag" with any piece of clothing it can find. When puppies are newly born, they have no teeth. At about four weeks of age, puppies of most breeds begin to develop their deciduous or baby teeth. They begin eating semi-solid food, fighting and biting with their litter mates, and learning discipline from their mother. As their new teeth come in, they inflict more pain on their mother's breasts, so her feeding sessions become less frequent and shorter. By six or eight weeks, the mother will start growling to warn her pups when they are fighting too roughly or hurting her as they nurse too much with their new teeth.

Puppies need to chew. It is a necessary part of their physical and mental development. They develop muscles and necessary life skills as they drag objects around, fight over possession, and vocalize alerts and warnings. Puppies chew on things to explore their world. They are using their sense of taste to determine what is food and what is not. How else can they tell an electrical cord from a lizard? At about four months of age, most puppies begin shedding their baby teeth. Often these teeth need some help to come out and make way for the permanent teeth. The incisors (front teeth) will be replaced first. Then, the adult canine or fang teeth erupt. When the baby tooth is not shed before the permanent tooth comes in, veterinarians call it a retained deciduous tooth. This condition will often cause gum infections by trapping hair and debris between the permanent tooth and the retained baby tooth. Nylafloss® is an excellent device for puppies to use. They can toss it, drag it, and chew on the many surfaces it presents. The baby teeth can catch in the nylon material, aiding in their removal. Puppies that have adequate chew toys will have less destructive behavior, develop more physically, and have less chance of retained deciduous teeth.

During the first year, your dog should be seen by your veterinarian at regular intervals. Your veterinarian will let you know when to bring in your puppy for vaccinations and parasite examinations. At each visit, your veterinarian should inspect the lips, teeth, and mouth as part of a complete physical examination. You should take some part in the maintenance of your dog's oral health. You should examine your dog's mouth weekly throughout his first year to make sure there are no sores, foreign objects, tooth problems, etc. If your dog drools excessively, shakes its head, or has bad breath, consult your veterinarian. By the time your dog is six months old, the permanent teeth are all in and plaque can start to accumulate on the tooth surfaces. This is when your dog needs to develop good dental-care habits to prevent calculus build-up on his teeth. Brushing is best. That is a fact that cannot be denied. However, some dogs do not like their teeth brushed regularly, or you may not be able to accomplish the task. In that case, you should consider a product that will help prevent plaque and calculus build-up.

*Nylon is the only material suitable for flossing human teeth. So why not get a chew toy that will enable you to interact with your Pekingese while it promotes dental health? As you play tug-of-war with a Nylafloss™, you'll be slowly pulling the nylon strand through your dog's teeth.*

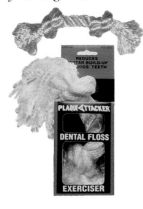

The Plaque Attackers® and Galileo Bone® are other excellent choices for the first three years of a dog's life. Their shapes make them interesting for the dog. As the dog chews on them, the solid polyurethane massages the gums which improves the blood circulation to the periodontal tissues. Projections on the chew devices increase the surface and are in contact with the tooth for more efficient cleaning. The unique shape and consistency prevent your dog from exerting excessive force on his own teeth or from breaking off pieces of the bone. If your dog is an aggressive chewer or weighs more than 55 pounds (25 kg), you should consider giving him a Nylabone®, the most durable chew product on the market.

The Gumabones ®, made by the Nylabone Company, is constructed of strong polyurethane, which is softer than nylon. Less powerful chewers prefer the Gumabones® to the Nylabones®. A super option for your dog is the Hercules Bone®, a uniquely shaped bone named after the great Olympian for its exception strength. Like all Nylabone products, they are specially scented to make them attractive to your dog. Ask your veterinarian about these bones and he will validate the good doctor's prescription: Nylabones® not only give your dog a good chewing workout but also help to save your dog's teeth (and even his life, as it protects him from possible fatal periodontal diseases).

By the time dogs are four years old, 75 percent of them have periodontal disease. It is the most common infection in dogs. Yearly examinations by your veterinarian are essential to maintaining your dog's good health. If your veterinarian detects periodontal disease, he or she may recommend a prophylactic cleaning. To do a thorough cleaning, it will be necessary to put your dog under anesthesia. With modern gas anesthetics and monitoring equipment, the procedure is pretty safe. Your veterinarian will scale the teeth with an ultrasound scaler or hand instrument. This removes the calculus from the teeth. If there are calculus deposits below the gum line, the veterinarian will plane the roots to make them smooth. After all of the calculus has been removed, the teeth are polished

*Raised dental tips on the surface of every Plaque Attacker™ bone help to combat plaque and tartar. Safe for aggressive chewers and ruggedly constructed to last, Plaque Attacker™ dental bones provide hours and hours of tooth-saving enjoyment.*

with pumice in a polishing cup. If any medical or surgical treatment is needed, it is done at this time. The final step would be fluoride treatment and your follow-up treatment at home. If the periodontal disease is advanced, the veterinarian may prescribe a medicated mouth rinse or antibiotics for use at home. Make sure your dog has safe, clean and attractive chew toys and treats. Chooz® treats are another way of using a consumable treat to help keep your dog's teeth clean.

Rawhide is the most popular of all materials for a dog to chew. This has never been good news to dog owners, because rawhide is inherently very dangerous for dogs. Thousands of dogs have died from rawhide, having swallowed the hide after it has become soft and mushy, only to cause stomach and intestinal blockage. A new rawhide product on the market has finally solved the problem of rawhide: molded Roar-Hide® from Nylabone. These are composed of processed, cut up, and melted American rawhide injected into your dog's favorite shape: a dog bone. These dog-safe devices smell and taste like rawhide but don't break up. The ridges on the bones help to fight tartar build-up on the teeth and they last ten times longer than the usual rawhide chews.

As your dog ages, professional examination and cleaning should become more frequent. The mouth should be inspected at least once a year. Your veterinarian may recommend visits every six months. In the geriatric patient, organs such as the heart, liver, and kidneys do not function as well as when they were young. Your veterinarian will probably want to test these organs' functions prior to using general anesthesia for dental cleaning. If your dog is a good chewer and you work closely with your veterinarian, your dog can keep all of his teeth all of his life. However, as your dog ages, his sense of smell, sight, and taste will diminish. He may not have the desire to chase, trap or chew his toys. He will also not have the energy to chew for long periods, as arthritis and periodontal disease make chewing painful. This will leave you with more responsibility for keeping his teeth clean and healthy. The dog that would not let you brush his teeth at one year of age, may let you brush his teeth now that he is ten years old.

If you train your dog with good chewing habits as a puppy, he will have healthier teeth throughout his life.

# TRAVELING with Your Dog

The earlier you start traveling with your new puppy or dog, the better. He needs to become accustomed to traveling. However, some dogs are nervous riders and become carsick easily. It is helpful if he starts with an empty stomach. Do not despair, as it will go better if you continue taking him with you on short fun rides. How would you feel if every time you rode in the car you stopped at the doctor's for an injection? You would soon dread that nasty car. Older dogs that tend to get carsick may have more of a problem adjusting to traveling. Those dogs that are having a serious problem may benefit from some medication prescribed by the veterinarian.

*Before any car excursion, be sure your Pekingese is allowed plenty of time outdoors to attend to his needs.*

Do give your dog a chance to relieve himself before getting into the car. It is a good idea to be prepared for a clean up with a leash, paper towels, bag and terry cloth towel. The safest place for your dog is in a fiberglass crate, although close confinement can promote carsickness in some dogs. If your dog is nervous you can try letting him ride on the seat next to you or in someone's lap.

An alternative to the crate would be to use a car harness made for dogs and/or a safety strap attached to the harness or collar. Whatever you do, do not let your dog ride in the back of

*If you take your Pekingese traveling with you often, he will quickly become accustomed to riding in the car.*

a pickup truck unless he is securely tied on a very short lead. I've seen trucks stop quickly and, even though the dog was tied, he fell out and was dragged.

Another advantage of the crate is that it is a safe place to leave him if you need to run into the store. Otherwise you wouldn't be able to leave the windows down. Keep in mind that while many dogs are overly protective in their crates, this may not be enough to deter dognappers. In some states it is against the law to leave a dog in the car unattended.

*Crates are a safe way for your dog to travel. The fiberglass crates are the safest for air travel, but the metal crates allow for better air circulation.*

Never leave a dog loose in the car wearing a collar and leash. More than one dog has killed himself by hanging. Do not let him put his head out an open window. Foreign debris can be blown into his eyes. When leaving your dog unattended in a car, consider the temperature. It can take less than five minutes to reach temperatures over 100 degrees Fahrenheit.

## TRIPS

Perhaps you are taking a trip. Give consideration to what is best for your dog—traveling with you or boarding. When traveling by car, van or motor home, you need to think ahead about locking your vehicle. In all probability you have many valuables in the car and do not wish to leave it unlocked. Perhaps most valuable and not replaceable is your dog. Give thought to securing your vehicle and providing adequate ventilation for him. Another consideration for you when traveling with your dog is medical problems that may arise and little inconveniences, such as exposure to external parasites. Some areas of the country are quite flea infested. You may want to carry flea spray with you. This is even a good idea when staying in motels. Quite possibly you are not the only occupant of the room.

Unbelievably many motels and even hotels do allow canine guests, even some very first-class ones. Gaines Pet Foods Corporation publishes *Touring With Towser*, a directory of domestic hotels and motels that accommodate guests with dogs. Their address is Gaines TWT, PO Box 5700, Kankakee, IL, 60902. Call ahead to any motel that you may be considering and see if they accept pets. Sometimes it is necessary to pay a deposit against room damage. The management may feel

*Your puppy's well-being is important to you, so be sure to inquire about airline and hotel regulations before making travel plans.*

reassured if you mention that your dog will be crated. If you do travel with your dog, take along plenty of baggies so that you can clean up after him. When we all do our share in cleaning up, we make it possible for motels to continue accepting our pets. As a matter of fact, you should practice cleaning up everywhere you take your dog.

Depending on where your are traveling, you may need an up-to-date health certificate issued by your veterinarian. It is good policy to take along your dog's medical information, which would include the name, address and phone number of your veterinarian, vaccination record, rabies certificate, and any medication he is taking.

## AIR TRAVEL

When traveling by air, you need to contact the airlines to check their policy. Usually you have to make arrangements up to a couple of weeks in advance for traveling with your dog. The airlines require your dog to travel in an airline approved fiberglass crate. Usually these can be purchased through the airlines but they are also readily available in most pet-supply stores. If your dog is not accustomed to a crate, then it is a good idea to get him acclimated to it before your trip. The day of the actual trip you should withhold water about one hour ahead of departure and no food for about 12 hours. The airlines generally have temperature restrictions, which do not allow pets to travel if it is either too cold or too hot. Frequently these restrictions are based on the temperatures at the departure and arrival airports. It's best to inquire about a health certificate. These usually need to be issued within ten days of departure. You should arrange for non-stop, direct flights and if a commuter plane should be involved, check to see if it will carry dogs. Some don't. The Humane Society of the United States has put together a tip sheet for airline traveling. You can receive a copy by sending a self-addressed stamped envelope to:

*Take along your dog's medical information with you when you travel, especially his vaccination record.*

The Humane Society of the United States
Tip Sheet
2100 L Street NW
Washington, DC 20037.

Regulations differ for traveling outside of the country and are sometimes changed without notice. Well in advance you need to write or call the appropriate consulate or agricultural department for instructions. Some countries have lengthy

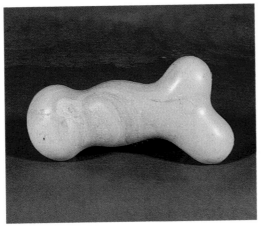

*The Galileo™ is the toughest nylon bone ever made. It is flavored to appeal to your Pekingese and has a relatively soft outer layer. It is a necessary chew toy and doggy pacifier.*

quarantines (six months), and countries differ in their rabies vaccination requirements. For instance, it may have to be given at least 30 days ahead of your departure.

Do make sure your dog is wearing proper identification including your name, phone number and city. You never know when you might be in an accident and separated from your dog. Or your dog could be frightened and somehow manage to escape and run away.

Another suggestion would be to carry in-case-of-emergency instructions. These would include the address and phone number of a relative or friend, your veterinarian's name, address and phone number, and your dog's medical information.

### BOARDING KENNELS

Perhaps you have decided that you need to board your dog. Your veterinarian can recommend a good boarding facility or possibly a pet sitter that will come to your house. It is customary for the boarding kennel to ask for proof of vaccination for the DHLPP, rabies and bordetella vaccine. The bordetella should have been given within six months of boarding. This is for your protection. If they do not ask for this proof I would not board at their kennel. Ask about flea control. Those dogs that suffer flea-bite allergy can get in trouble at a boarding kennel. Unfortunately boarding kennels are limited on how much they are able to do.

For more information on pet sitting, contact NAPPS:
National Association of Professional Pet Sitters
1200 G Street, NW
Suite 760
Washington, DC 20005.

*This little Pekingese looks ready for adventure— now the only question is, who's going to pull the wagon?*

Some pet clinics have technicians that pet sit and technicians that board clinic patients in their homes. This may be an alternative for you. Ask your veterinarian if they have an employee that can help you. There is a definite advantage of having a technician care for your dog, especially if

*A reputable boarding kennel will require that dogs receive the vaccination for kennel cough no less than two weeks before their scheduled stay.*

*If you decide to bring your Pekingese with you when you travel, bring along some familiar things, like his bed and toys, to make him feel more at home.*

your dog is on medication or is a senior citizen.

You can write for a copy of *Traveling With Your Pet* from ASPCA, Education Department, 441 E. 92nd Street, New York, NY 10128.

# IDENTIFICATION and Finding the Lost Dog

There are several ways of identifying your dog. The old standby is a collar with dog license, rabies, and ID tags. Unfortunately collars have a way of being separated from the dog and tags fall off. We're not suggesting you shouldn't use a collar and tags. If they stay intact and on the dog, they are the quickest way of identification.

For several years owners have been tattooing their dogs. Some tattoos use a number with a registry. Here lies the problem because there are several registries to check. If you wish to tattoo, use your social security number. The humane shelters have the means to trace it. It is usually done on the inside of the rear thigh. The area is first shaved and numbed. There is no pain, although a few dogs do not like the buzzing sound. Occasionally tattooing is not legible and needs to be redone.

*The newest method of identification is microchipping. The microchip is no bigger than a grain of rice.*

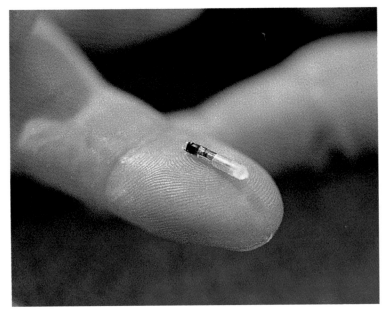

*Pekingese like to be active. Provide yours with a safe outdoor enclosure for playtime.*

The newest method of identification is microchipping. The microchip is a computer chip that is no larger than a grain of rice. The veterinarian implants it by injection between the shoulder blades. The dog feels no discomfort. If your dog is lost and picked up by the humane society, they can trace you by scanning the microchip, which has its own code. Microchip scanners are friendly to other brands of microchips and their registries. The microchip comes with a dog tag saying the dog is microchipped. It is the safest way of identifying your dog.

## FINDING THE LOST DOG

I am sure you will agree that there would be little worse than losing your dog. Responsible pet owners rarely lose their dogs. They do not let their dogs run free because they don't want harm to come to them. Not only that but in most, if not all, states there is a leash law.

Beware of fenced-in yards. They can be a hazard. Dogs find ways to escape either over or under the fence. Another fast exit is through the gate that perhaps the neighbor's child left unlocked.

Below is a list that hopefully will be of help to you if you need it. Remember don't give up, keep looking. Your dog is worth your efforts.

*Make sure you have a clear recent picture of your Pekingese to distribute in case he becomes lost.*

1. Contact your neighbors and put flyers with a photo on it in their mailboxes. Information you should include would be the dog's name, breed, sex, color, age, source of identification, when your dog was last seen and where, and your name and phone numbers. It may be helpful to say the dog needs medical care. Offer a *reward*.
2. Check all local shelters daily. It is also possible for your dog to be picked up away from home and end up in an out-of-the-way shelter. Check these too. Go in person. It is not good enough to call. Most shelters are limited on the time they can hold dogs then they are put up for adoption or euthanized. There is the possibility that your dog will not make it to the shelter for several days. Your dog could have been wandering or someone may have tried to keep him.
3. Notify all local veterinarians. Call and send flyers.
4. Call your breeder. Frequently breeders are contacted when one of their breed is found.
5. Contact the rescue group for your breed.
6. Contact local schools—children may have seen your dog.
7. Post flyers at the schools, groceries, gas stations, convenience stores, veterinary clinics, groomers and any other place that will allow them.
8. Advertise in the newspaper.
9. Advertise on the radio.

# BEHAVIOR and Canine Communication

Studies of the human/animal bond point out the importance of the unique relationships that exist between people and their pets. Those of us who share our lives with pets understand the special part they play through companionship, service and protection. For many, the pet/owner bond goes beyond simple companionship; pets are often considered members of the family. A leading pet food manufacturer recently conducted a nationwide survey of pet owners to gauge just how important pets were in their lives. Here's what they found:

- 76 percent allow their pets to sleep on their beds
- 78 percent think of their pets as their children
- 84 percent display photos of their pets, mostly in their homes

*Dogs are a very important part of their owner's lives, and the bond between humans and animals is a strong one.*

*A lot can be learned about a Pekingese's behavior and attitude simply by observing his body language. This little guy looks relaxed and calm.*

• 84 percent think that their pets react to their own emotions
• 100 percent talk to their pets
• 97 percent think that their pets understand what they're saying

Are you surprised?

Senior citizens show more concern for their own eating habits when they have the responsibility of feeding a dog. Seeing that their dog is routinely exercised encourages the owner to think of schedules that otherwise may seem unimportant to the senior citizen. The older owner may be arthritic and feeling poorly but with responsibility for his dog he has a reason to get up and get moving. It is a big plus if his dog is an attention seeker who will demand such from his owner.

*Many people thrive on the devoted companionship a Pekingese can provide. These two buddies surely agree!*

Over the last couple of decades, it has been shown that pets relieve the stress of those who lead busy lives. Owning a pet has been known to lessen the occurrence of heart attack and stroke.

Many single folks thrive on the companionship of a dog. Lifestyles are very different from a long time ago, and today more individuals seek the single life. However, they receive fulfillment from owning a dog.

Most likely the majority of our dogs live in family environments. The companionship they provide is well worth the effort involved. In my opinion, every child should have the opportunity to have a family dog. Dogs teach responsibility through understanding their care, feelings and even respecting their life cycles. Frequently those children who have not been exposed to dogs grow up afraid of dogs, which isn't good. Dogs sense timidity and some will take advantage of the situation.

Today more dogs are serving as service dogs. Since the origination of the Seeing Eye dogs years ago, we now have trained hearing dogs. Also dogs are trained to provide service

for the handicapped and are able to perform many different tasks for their owners. Search and Rescue dogs, with their handlers,

*There are many predicaments your Peke can get into in the great outdoors. Always supervise him closely when outside.*

are sent throughout the world to assist in recovery of disaster victims. They are life savers.

Therapy dogs are very popular with nursing homes, and some hospitals even allow them to visit. The inhabitants truly look forward to their visits. They wanted and were allowed to have visiting dogs in their beds to hold and love.

Nationally there is a Pet Awareness Week to educate students and others about the value and basic care of our pets. Many countries take an even greater interest in their pets than Americans do. In those countries the pets are allowed to accompany their owners into restaurants and shops, etc. In the US this freedom is only available to our service dogs. Even so we think very highly of the human/animal bond.

## CANINE BEHAVIOR

Canine behavior problems are the number-one reason for pet owners to dispose of their dogs, either through new homes, humane shelters or euthanasia. Unfortunately there are too many owners who are unwilling to devote the necessary time to properly train their dogs. On the other hand, there are those who not only are concerned about inherited

*A stable, even-tempered Pekingese is one that is neither fearful nor aggressive.*

*Puppies will find mischief whenever possible! You will have to play the role of pack leader in order to teach your Peke appropriate behavior.*

health problems but are also aware of the dog's mental stability.

You may realize that a breed and his group relatives (i.e., sporting, hounds, etc.) show tendencies to behavioral characteristics. An experienced breeder can acquaint you with his breed's personality. Unfortunately many breeds are labeled with poor temperaments when actually the breed as a whole is not affected but only a small percentage of individuals within the breed.

Inheritance and environment contribute to the dog's behavior. Some naïve people suggest inbreeding as the cause of bad temperaments. Inbreeding only results in poor behavior if the ancestors carry the trait. If there are excellent temperaments behind the dogs, then inbreeding will promote good temperaments in the offspring. Did you ever consider that inbreeding is what sets the characteristics of a breed? A purebred dog is the end result of inbreeding. This does not spare the mixed-breed dog from the same problems. Mixed-breed dogs frequently are the offspring of purebred dogs.

Not too many decades ago most of our dogs led a different lifestyle than what is prevalent today. Usually mom stayed home so the dog had human companionship and someone to discipline him if needed. Not much was expected from the dog. Today's mom works and everyone's life is at a much faster pace.

The dog may have to adjust to being a "weekend" dog. The family is gone all day during the week, and the dog is left to his own devices for entertainment. Some dogs sleep all day waiting for their family to come home and others become wigwam wreckers if given the opportunity. Crates do ensure the safety of the dog and the house. However, he could become a physically and emotionally cripple if he doesn't get enough exercise and attention. We still appreciate and want the companionship of our dogs although we expect more from them. In many cases we tend to forget dogs are just that–*dogs* and not human beings.

## SOCIALIZING AND TRAINING

Many prospective puppy buyers lack experience regarding the proper socialization and training needed to develop the type of pet we all desire. In the first 18 months, training does take some work. It is easier to start proper training before there is a problem that needs to be corrected.

*Most Pekingese become members of the family and must learn to conform to the rules of the household. It seems like this little guy knows he needs to wipe his feet when coming in from outside!*

The initial work begins with the breeder. The breeder should start socializing the puppy at five to six weeks of age and cannot let up. Human socializing is critical up through 12 weeks of age and likewise important during the following months. The litter should be left together during the first few weeks but it is necessary to separate them by ten weeks of age. Leaving them together after that time will increase competition for litter

*If you take the time to teach your Pekingese proper behavior as a puppy, he will be a model canine citizen in adulthood.*

dominance. If puppies are not socialized with people by 12 weeks of age, they will be timid in later life.

*Although some traits are inherited within a breed, every Pekingese is an individual. These intrepid snow explorers agree!*

The eight- to ten-week age period is a fearful time for puppies. They need to be handled very gently around children and adults. There should be no harsh discipline during this time. Starting at

14 weeks of age, the puppy begins the juvenile period, which ends when he reaches sexual maturity around six to 14 months of age. During the juvenile period he needs to be introduced to strangers (adults, children and other dogs) on the home property. At sexual maturity he will begin to bark at strangers and become more protective. Males start to lift their legs to urinate but if you desire you can inhibit this behavior by walking your boy on leash away from trees, shrubs, fences, etc.

*Your Pekingese is happiest when being loved and enjoyed. Although correction will sometimes be necessary, it will all prove worthwhile in the end.*

Perhaps you are thinking about an older puppy. You need to inquire about the puppy's social experience. If he has lived in a kennel, he may have a hard time adjusting to people and environmental stimuli. Assuming he has had a good social upbringing, there are advantages to an older puppy.

Training includes puppy kindergarten and a minimum of one to two basic training classes. During these classes you will learn how to dominate your youngster. This is especially important if you own a large breed of dog. It is somewhat harder, if not nearly impossible, for some owners to be the Alpha figure when their dog towers over them. You will be taught how to properly restrain your dog. This concept is important. Again it puts you in the Alpha position. All dogs need to be restrained many times during their lives. Believe it or not, some of our worst offenders are the eight-week-old puppies that are brought to our clinic. They need to be gently restrained for a nail trim but the way they carry on you would

think we were killing them. In comparison, their vaccination is a "piece of cake." When

*With the proper supervision, your Pekingese should be encouraged to explore his surroundings whenever possible.*

we ask dogs to do something that is not agreeable to them, then their worst comes out. Life will be easier for your dog if you expose him at a young age to the necessities of life—proper behavior and restraint.

## UNDERSTANDING THE DOG'S LANGUAGE

Most authorities agree that the dog is a descendent of the wolf. The dog and wolf have similar traits. For instance both are pack oriented and prefer not to be isolated for long periods of time. Another characteristic is that the dog, like the wolf, looks to the leader—Alpha—for direction. Both the wolf and the dog communicate through body language, not only within their pack but with outsiders.

Every pack has an Alpha figure. The dog looks to you, or should look to you, to be that leader. If your dog doesn't receive the proper training and guidance, he very well may replace you as Alpha. This would be a serious problem and is certainly a disservice to your dog.

Eye contact is one way the Alpha wolf keeps order within his pack. You are Alpha so you must establish eye contact with your puppy. Obviously your puppy will have to look at you. Practice eye contact even if you need to hold his head for five to ten seconds at a time. You can give him a treat as a reward. Make

*Behavior and health problems can be passed down from generation to generation, so be sure to check your puppy's lineage very carefully.*

*Although this Pekingese can hardly be blamed for jumping up on the couch to admire his likeness, if you allow bad habits like sitting on the furniture to develop, they can be very hard to break.*

sure your eye contact is gentle and not threatening. Later, if he has been naughty, it is permissible to give him a long, penetrating look. There are some older dogs that never learned eye contact as puppies and cannot accept eye contact. You should avoid eye contact with these dogs since they feel threatened and will retaliate as such.

## BODY LANGUAGE

The play bow, when the forequarters are down and the hindquarters are elevated, is an invitation to play. Puppies play fight, which helps them learn the acceptable limits of biting. This is necessary for later in their lives. Nevertheless, an owner may be falsely reassured by the playful nature of his dog's aggression. Playful aggression toward another dog or human may be an indication of serious aggression in the future. Owners should never play fight or play tug-of-war with any dog that is inclined to be dominant.

Signs of submission are:
1. Avoids eye contact.
2. Active submission—the dog crouches down, ears back and the tail is lowered.
3. Passive submission—the dog rolls on his side with his hindlegs in the air and frequently urinates.

Signs of dominance are:
1. Makes eye contact.
2. Stands with ears up, tail up and the hair raised on his neck.
3. Shows dominance over another dog by standing at right angles over it.

Dominant dogs tend to behave in characteristic ways such as:
1. The dog may be unwilling to move from his place (i.e., reluctant to give up the sofa if the owner wants to sit there).
2. He may not part with toys or objects in his mouth and may show possessiveness with his food bowl.
3. He may not respond quickly to commands.
4. He may be disagreeable for grooming and dislikes to be petted.

Dogs are popular because of their sociable nature. Those that have contact with humans during the first 12 weeks of life regard them as a member of their own species—their pack. All dogs have the potential for both dominant and submissive behavior. Only through experience and training do they learn to whom it is appropriate to show which behavior. Not all dogs are concerned with dominance but owners need to be aware of that potential. It is wise for the owner to establish his dominance early on.

*Although the regal bearing of the Pekingese may cause them to appear standoffish at times, they are loving and affectionate pets.*

A human can express dominance or submission toward a dog in the following ways:

1. Meeting the dog's gaze signals dominance. Averting the gaze signals submission. If the dog growls or threatens, averting the gaze is the first avoiding action to take—it may prevent attack. It is important to establish eye contact in the puppy. The older dog that has not been exposed to eye contact may see it as a threat and will not be willing to submit.

*Your Pekingese should never be forced into a situation he finds frightening. Respect his feelings and allow him time to acclimate to the situation.*

*An unwillingness to give up his toys may signal that your dog is displaying dominant tendencies. Your Peke must always know that you are the boss.*

2. Being taller than the dog signals dominance; being lower signals submission. This is why, when

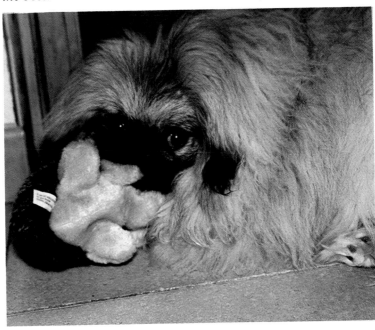

attempting to make friends with a strange dog or catch the runaway, one should kneel down to his level. Some owners see their dogs become dominant when allowed on the furniture or on the bed. Then he is at the owner's level.

3. An owner can gain dominance by ignoring all the dog's social initiatives. The owner pays attention to the dog only when he obeys a command.

No dog should be allowed to achieve dominant status over any adult or child. Ways of preventing are as follows:

*It is important to remember that your Pekingese wants to please you and with patience, will learn what you have to teach him.*

1. Handle the puppy gently, especially during the three- to four-month period.
2. Let the children and adults handfeed him and teach him to take food without lunging or grabbing.
3. Do not allow him to chase children or joggers.
4. Do not allow him to jump on people or mount their legs. Even females may be inclined to mount. It is not only a male habit.
5. Do not allow him to growl for any reason.
6. Don't participate in wrestling or tug-of-war games.
7. Don't physically punish puppies for aggressive behavior. Restrain him from repeating the infraction and teach an alternative behavior. Dogs should earn everything they receive from their owners. This would include sitting to receive petting or treats, sitting before going out the door and sitting to receive the collar and leash. These types of exercises reinforce the owner's dominance.

Young children should never be left alone with a dog. It is important that children

*Your Pekingese must be taught to behave. The result will be a well-mannered and amiable companion.*

learn some basic obedience commands so they have some control over the dog. They will gain the respect of their dog.

## FEAR

One of the most common problems dogs experience is being fearful. Some dogs are more afraid than others. On the lesser side, which is sometimes humorous to watch, dogs can be afraid of a strange object. They act silly when something is out of place in the house. We call this problem perceptive intelligence. He realizes the abnormal within his known environment. He does not react the same way in strange environments since he does not know what is normal.

On the more serious side is a fear of people. This can result in backing off, seeking his own space, and saying "leave me alone" or it can result in an aggressive behavior that may lead to challenging the person. Respect that the dog wants to be left alone and give him time to come forward. If you approach the cornered dog, he may resort to snapping. If you leave him alone, he may decide to come forward, which should be rewarded with a treat.

Some dogs may initially be too fearful to take treats. In these cases it is helpful to make sure the dog hasn't

*These two Pekingese have clearly been well socialized—they don't mind sharing a pillow at all!*

*Eye contact is an extremely important part of your relationship with your Pekingese. It will help to establish you as pack leader in your dog's mind.*

eaten for about 24 hours. Being a little hungry encourages him to accept the treats, especially if they are of the "gourmet" variety.

Dogs can be afraid of numerous things, including loud noises and thunderstorms. Invariably the owner rewards (by comforting) the dog when he shows signs of fearfulness. When your dog is frightened, direct his attention to something else and act happy. Don't dwell on his fright.

## AGGRESSION

Some different types of aggression are: predatory, defensive, dominance, possessive, protective, fear induced, noise provoked, "rage" syndrome (unprovoked aggression), maternal, and aggression directed toward other dogs. Aggression is the most common behavioral problem encountered. Protective breeds are expected to be more aggressive than others but with the proper upbringing they can make very dependable companions. You need to be able to read your dog.

Many factors contribute to aggression including genetics and environment. An improper environment, which may include the living conditions, lack of social life, excessive punishment, being attacked or frightened by an aggressive dog, etc., can all influence a dog's behavior. Even spoiling him and giving too much praise may be detrimental. Isolation and the lack of human contact or exposure to frequent teasing by children or adults also can ruin a good dog.

Lack of direction, fear, or confusion lead to aggression in those dogs that are so inclined. Any obedience exercise, even the sit and down, can direct the dog and overcome fear and/or confusion. Every dog should learn these commands as a youngster, and there should be periodic reinforcement.

When a dog is showing signs of aggression, you should speak calmly (no screaming or hysterics) and firmly give a command that he understands, such as the sit. As soon as your dog obeys, you have assumed your dominant position. Aggression presents a problem because there may be danger to others. Sometimes it is an emotional issue. Owners may consciously or unconsciously encourage their dog's aggression. Other owners show responsibility by accepting the problem and taking measures to keep it under control. The owner is responsible for his dog's actions, and it is not wise to take a chance on someone being bitten, especially a child. Euthanasia is the solution for some owners and in severe cases this may be the best choice. However, few dogs are that dangerous and very few are that much of a threat to their owners. If caution is exercised and professional help is gained early on, most cases can be controlled.

Some authorities recommend feeding a lower protein (less than 20 percent) diet. They believe this can aid in reducing aggression. If the dog loses weight, then vegetable oil can be added. Veterinarians and behaviorists are having some success with pharmacology. In many cases treatment is possible and can improve the situation.

If you have done everything according to "the book" regarding training and socializing and are still having a behavior problem, don't procrastinate. It is important that the problem gets attention before it is out of hand. It is estimated that 20 percent of a veterinarian's time may be devoted to dealing with problems before they become so intolerable that the dog is separated from his home and owner. If your veterinarian isn't able to help, he should refer you to a behaviorist.

# SUGGESTED READING

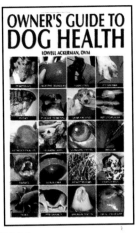

TS-257
*Choosing A Dog for Life*
*Andrew DePrisco and James*
*Johnson*
*384 pages, over 700 full-color photos*

TS-214
*Owner's Guide to Dog Health*
*Dr. Lowell Ackerman, DVM*
*224 pages, over 190 full-color photos*

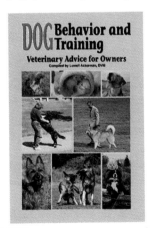

TS-252
*Dog Behavior and Training*
*Edited by Dr. Lowell Ackerman,*
*DVM*
*292 pages, over 200 full-color photos*

TS-249
*Skin and Coat Care for Your Dog*
*Dr. Lowell Ackerman, DVM*
*224 pages, 265 full-color photos.*

# INDEX

Adolescence, 48
Aggression, 157
Agility, 103
Air travel, 131
American Kennel Club, 11, 24, 34, 88, 89,105
Bathing, 68
Boarding kennels, 134
Body language, 151
Bordetella, 111
Breeders, 30
Breeding, 20
Canadian Kennel Club, 88, 89
Canine good citizen, 99
Chaou Ching-Ur, 11
Cheyletiella, 119
China, 6, 9, 10
China War, 10
Coat, 15, 60
—adult, 66
—puppy, 61
Coccidiosis, 115
Come, 79
Conformation, 91
Coronavirus, 111
Crates, 71
—training, 71
—travel, 131
Demodectic mange, 119
Diet sheet, 43
Diet, 51, 54
Distemper, 41, 110
Dog food, 51
Dominance, 152
Down, 83, 90
Dunne, Lieutenent, 10
Exercise, 57
External parasites, 116
Eye care, 56
Fear, 156
Feeding, 50
Fiennes, Richard and Alice, 6

Fitzroy, Sir George, 10
Fleas, 116
Franco-British Invasion, 10
Giardiasis, 115
Ha pa dogs, 7
Handling, 57
Hay, Lord John, 10
Health guarantee, 44
Health record, 41
Heartworm disease, 116
Heel, 86, 90
Hepatitis, 41, 110
Hookworms, 113
Housebreaking, 71
Immunizations, 108
Inoculations, 41
Intestinal parasites, 113-115
Junior showmanship, 98
Kennel Club, The, 11, 88, 89
Kennel cough, 111
Leash training, 78
Leptospirosis, 41, 110
Looty, 10
Lyme disease, 111
Mange, 119
Microchipping, 136
Ming dynasty, 9
Nail trimming, 66
Natural History of Dogs, The, 6
Neutering, 20, 120
No, 77
Nutrition, 50
Obedience, 101
Parasites, 113-116
—external, 116
—intestinal, 113-115
Parvovirus, 41, 110
Pedigree, 41
Pekingese Club of America, Inc., 11, 24

Pekingese Club, The, 11
Performance tests, 104
Periodontal disease, 126
Personality, 21
Puppy kindergarten, 89
Puppy, 32-34
—selection, 33, 34
Rabies, 41, 111
Recall, 91
Registration certificate, 41, 42
Roundworms, 113
Sarcoptic mange, 119
Sit, 81, 90
Socialization, 45, 58, 146
Spaying, 20, 120
Stay, 81
Submission, 152
Supplementation, 52
T'ang of Downshire, 11
Tapeworms, 115
Tattooing, 136
Temperament, 45
Therapy dogs, 88
Tibet, 6, 7
Ticks, 119
Toy Spaniel Club, 11
Training, 76, 146
—basic, 76
—crate, 71
—leash, 78
Tzu Hsi, Dowager Empress, 9
Versatility, 87
Veterinarian, 106, 108, 113
—annual visit, 113
—first check up, 106
—physical exam, 108
Victoria, Queen, 10
Weather, 54
Whipworms, 114